Andreae

AND THE

FORMULA OF CONCORD

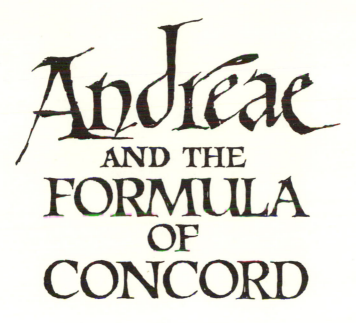

Andreae
AND THE
FORMULA
OF
CONCORD

Six Sermons on the Way to Lutheran Unity

❧

ROBERT KOLB

Publishing House
St. Louis

Concordia Publishing House, St. Louis, Missouri
Copyright © 1977 Concordia Publishing House
MANUFACTURED IN THE UNITED STATES OF AMERICA

Library of Congress Cataloging in Publication Data

Kolb, Robert, 1941-
      Andreae and the Formula of concord.

      Confession and brief explanation of certain disputed articles, by J. Andreae: p.
      Six Christian sermons, by J. Andreae: p.
      Includes bibliographical references.
      1. Andreae, Jakob, 1528-1590. 2. Lutheran Church. Formula of concord. 3. Lutheran
Church—Clergy—Biography. 4. Clergy—Germany—Biography. I. Andreae, Jakob, 1528-
1590. Bekenntnis und kurze Erklärung etlicher zwiespaltiger Artikel. English. 1977. II. Andreae,
Jakob, 1528-1590.
Sechs christlicher Predig. English. 1977.
III. Title.
BX8080.A55K64   230'.4'10924 [B]   76-28542
ISBN 0-570-03741-7

CONTENTS

PREFACE

This study of Jakob Andreae's *Six Christian Sermons* of 1573 was made possible through a fellowship awarded me by the Center for Reformation Research under a grant from the Literature Commission of The Lutheran Church—Missouri Synod. The commission's generous financial support made possible the completion of the translation and the examination of the historical context in which the *Sermons* were written. I must express my special thanks to those members of the commission who offered encouragement and assistance, Professors John W. Klotz, Robert D. Preus, and Wilbert H. Rosin.

Professors Carl S. Meyer and Arthur Carl Piepkorn contributed a great deal to this study, and I acknowledge my debt to them both with pleasure. Both men shared a dedication to the study of the Lutheran Confessions which inspired me as a student and which supported me during my research on this project. Dr. Meyer conceived the project and guided initial work on it, and Dr. Piepkorn freely shared his insights into the period with me during the year between Dr. Meyer's death and his own.

I am grateful to Prof. Herbert J. A. Bouman for reading the manuscript and to four student assistants at the Center for Reformation Research, Robert Rosin, Jon Imme, Gregory Barth, and David Lumpp, who provided valuable assistance; and I am very thankful to my wife Pauline for encouragement and suggestions along the road between my first reading of the German text of the *Sermons* and the final typing of its English translation, also a part of her contribution.

Furthermore, my doctoral adviser, Dr. Robert M. Kingdon of the University of Wisconsin, deserves mention, for under his guidance I prepared my dissertation, "Nikolaus von Amsdorf, Knight of God and Exile of Christ. Piety and Polemic in the Wake of Luther" (1973); much of my understanding of the period, as reflected in this introduction, comes from my work with Dr. Kingdon.

The notes accompanying the introduction and translation offer some primary and secondary bibliography, but they mention only a few of the

16th-century documents and 20th-century analyses of the events and ideas of the German Late Reformation. I have tried to point the reader to the pertinent materials available in English and have attempted to whet the appetite of some for delving into the primary sources and classic German studies. For more complete references and bibliographies the reader is referred to such studies and to the standard works of the history of dogma which treat this period.

INTRODUCTION

Jakob Andreae

Jakob Andreae[1] was not, from many points of view, the ideal ambassador of peace and reconciliation in the midst of the turmoil that beset German Lutheranism in the third quarter of the 16th-century. Although it was not unusual for Evangelical pastors of his day to have risen from low birth, Andreae's opponents delighted in snide observations about the humble origins of this son of a smithy. Apparently somewhat abrupt and acerbic, he had a way of antagonizing the theologians he came to reconcile. During the early years of his efforts toward concord he managed to arouse the suspicion of both the major opposing parties in north Germany, the Gnesio-Lutherans and the Philippists, because he seemed to favor first one and then the other as he struggled to formulate a unifying document. Degradation, defeat, rejection, and rancor pursued Andreae as he strove to create an atmosphere of mutual trust and confessional agreement among the followers of Luther. He plunged into complicated theological problems without being a great theologian himself. He was instead first of all a pastor; as a thinker he was something of a simplifier.

Andreae capitalized on a wide-felt longing for ecclesiastical peace and harmony, shared by princes, theologians, and lay people. He combined pastoral concern, skill at stating convincingly a simple version of a complicated controversy, dogged persistence, and an ability to put up with personal abuse and dramatic defeat to achieve his final accomplishment, the Formula of Concord of 1577. The moral, financial, and political support of several Evangelical princes provided the motive force that kept Andreae's mission alive for over a decade. Yet princely power alone could not have imposed a settlement on cantankerous theologians, convinced in their consciences that truth must prevail. It was Andreae who was able to use both princely power and the power of the Lutheran longing for concord to construct the settlement of the Formula of Concord. While others had to join the effort for it to reach fruition, it was Andreae who, through his commitment to a pastoral and Scriptural path to harmony, was able to initiate the final movement toward Lutheran theological concord in the last third of the 16th century. The story of that initial push, which is essentially the story of Andreae's *Six Christian Sermons on the Divisions Among the Theologians of the Augsburg Confession,* is laid out here.

The Education of a Pastor

When Jakob Andreae was born, on March 25, 1528, his native town, Waiblingen, was, with the rest of the dukedom of Wuerttemberg, under the control of the Austrian house of Hapsburg. Jakob was six years old when the forces of Philip of Hesse restored Ulrich, duke of Wuerttemberg, to power in his lands in 1534. Part of Ulrich's obligation to the Evangelical landgrave of Hesse was the introduction of Evangelical church reform to his lands, so that at the very time when Andreae began his formal learning he became, like all other Wuerttembergers, an Evangelical. As the son of a smith, Andreae enjoyed the right to education in his hometown, but his father was too poor to support advanced education for Jakob. Thus in 1539 Andreae left Latin school to begin an apprenticeship as a carpenter. However, his abilities had been recognized in the Waiblingen school, and the mayor of the town arranged for a ducal scholarship to enable Jakob to continue his studies.

At Pentecost 1539 Andreae came to the ducal residence town of Stuttgart and enrolled in its preparatory school. Two years later, at age 13, he matriculated at the University of Tuebingen; again the continuation of his formal studies was dependent on financial support from the duke. After four years of study in the liberal arts, he advanced to the study of theology in 1545.

Compared to other Evangelical theological faculties, particularly that at Wittenberg, the one at Tuebingen was not at all strong, and Andreae's theological studies did not last long. Wuerttemberg needed Evangelical pastors, so Andreae assumed the duties of deacon at the Hospital Church in Stuttgart just one year after he had begun to study theology. His antagonists later called him a theological lightweight because he had had so little formal theological training. However, theology was for Andreae a practical discipline, and many of his theological endeavors were dedicated to meeting and solving pastoral problems.

The Superintendent of Goeppingen:
Ducal Emissary and Adviser

In 1546 Andreae assumed not only pastoral but also conjugal duties, marrying Anna, the daughter of a citizen of Tuebingen, Johann Entringer.

With hardly more than a year's parish experience behind him, Andreae faced a rapidly changing world. After the defeat of the Evangelical forces at Muehlberg on April 24, 1547, the forces of Emperor Charles V moved to impose his interim religious settlement upon Evangelicals throughout the Holy Roman Empire. He was able to do this somewhat effectively in southern Germany, including Wuerttemberg. Andreae alone among the Evangelical pastors in Stuttgart remained at his post when the Spanish occupation forces of the emperor began to implement the Augsburg Interim in the city in November 1548. Duke Ulrich transferred his young dependent to Tuebingen soon thereafter, however, to help him avoid arrest. In Tuebingen he preached in a chapel while Roman Catholic priests held Mass at the city churches. While serving as a catechist for two congregations, Andreae again enrolled at the university to work on his doctorate. Particularly weak because of the imperial occupation, the theological faculty at Tuebingen around 1550 had little except a degree to offer Andreae, although in 1551 Martin Frecht and Jakob Beurlin began the rebuilding of the Evangelical faculty.

During his doctoral studies Andreae began his rise to prominence as a ducal ecclesiastical adviser. Johann Brenz, reformer of the imperial city of Schwaebisch Hall, located at the northern edge of Duke Ulrich's domains, had been wooed by the duke for a number of years and finally joined the ducal staff after Ulrich gave him protection from persecution during the imperial occupation and the imposition of the Interim. Brenz influenced Andreae's theology and shaped his attitudes toward ecclesiastical practices during their 20-year association.

Duke Ulrich died in 1550 and was succeeded by his son Christoph, who insisted that Andreae complete his doctoral program and then accept a call to a pastorate in his lands. In early 1553 Andreae assumed the duties of superintendent of the churches in the town of Goeppingen. In that capacity he not only served as pastor of a congregation but also supervised the development and practice of church life in the town and its surrounding villages.

When Andreae came to Goeppingen, less than 20 years after the

Reformation had been introduced there, the church was still in the process of transforming medieval ecclesiastical discipline and practice into something Evangelical. In the development of new forms for his churches Andreae became embroiled in a small dispute with his friend Johann Brenz and the ducal ecclesiastical staff in Stuttgart. With his brother-in-law Caspar Leyser, also a pastor, Andreae promoted plans for the exercise of authority and discipline in the church of Wuerttemberg that were similar to those used in Geneva by John Calvin. Both men had corresponded with Calvin and had high regard for his attempt to formulate a mediating position between theologians from Zurich and Wittenberg concerning the Lord's Supper. The pastor of Goeppingen was particularly attracted to Calvin's concept of ecclesiastical organization, centered as it was in the hands of the town leadership. Brenz was committed instead to a centralized church for the ducal lands, with a larger concentration of ecclesiastical power in Stuttgart. Duke Christoph at first tended to support his young whiz kid in Goeppingen but was won around to Brenz's viewpoint rather easily, especially since it coincided more closely with his own plans for the consolidation of power in the hands of the prince and his counselors.[2] Andreae's case was discussed in a synod of the church of Wuerttemberg; his proposals were rejected. This incident demonstrates that, though he was extremely grateful to his duke for financial support for his education, the young Andreae was not just a compliant tool who shrank from causing his duke and his superiors any aggravation at all. On the other hand, he did not press his position once the decision had gone against him, and this minor disagreement did not damage his relationship with either Brenz or Christoph.

The duke recognized Andreae's talents and used him already in 1556 on a visitation within his lands to help reorganize church life along Evangelical lines. The same year he was sent to the county of Hohenlohe, north of Goeppingen, and to the county of Wiesensteig on similar assignments. Later in 1556 he was invited to join two theologians from ducal Saxony and one from the Palatinate in organizing the reformation of the church of Baden-Durlach, west of Wuerttemberg. On this assignment he first encountered the stubbornness and suspicion of Gnesio-Lutheran theologians, for the ducal Saxon representatives, Maximilian Moerlin and Johann Stoessel, delayed their joint efforts with questions about the stance of the Wuerttembergers in regard to a number of key questions.

Although Christoph had to reject invitations to loan Andreae to some princes, including the duke of Prussia, he did send the pastor from Goeppingen to the county of Oettingen in 1558, to the imperial city of Hagenau in 1565, and to the duchy of Braunschweig-Wolfenbuettel in 1568, as well as to other villages and towns inside and outside his domains, to assist in reforming ecclesiastical life and organizing the Evangelical church in those places.

Within Wuerttemberg Andreae's stature as a leading theologian steadily increased as he entered his 30s. He participated in the synod of Stuttgart in December 1559, in which Brenz' understanding of Christ's ubiquity was defended in the official "Confession and Report of the Theologians and Ministers in the Princedom of Wuerttemberg, Concerning the True Presence of the Body and Blood of Christ in the Holy Supper." In his agreement with Brenz on the ubiquity of Christ's human nature Andreae was drawing a very clear line between himself and Calvin on the doctrine of the Lord's Supper even though he had made a serious effort not long before the synod to formulate a position on which Lutherans and Calvinists could agree. The synod had been called to deal with the case of a Wuerttemberg clergyman, Bartholomaeus Hagen, who tended toward a Calvinist understanding of Christ's presence in the Sacrament. Andreae was the duke's official representative and strove to bring Hagen into agreement with the strict Lutheran position of the duke, Brenz, and the other ducal counselors. By declaring in a formal confession their commitment to the doctrine of Christ's ubiquity, Andreae and his colleagues secured the Lutheran doctrine of the Lord's Supper in Wuerttemberg and raised an issue which would lie at the heart of Andreae's difficulties with the theological faculty at Wittenberg a decade later.

Duke Christoph's family held the county of Montbeliard in France, and in part because of this the duke noted religious developments inside France with genuine interest. Initially favorable toward the Calvinist reformers in France, Christoph cooled toward them at the end of the 1550s, shortly before the outbreak of religious warfare in France. He increased the political distance between himself and the Calvinists at the same time he was defining the doctrinal position of his church in a strictly Lutheran way. Nonetheless, his interest in the French situation remained alive, and he responded warmly to an invitation from the Roman Catholic duke of Guise to send representatives to the Colloquy of Poissy, which was called in 1561 to explore the possibility of agreement between the Calvinist and Roman Catholic parties in France. The Guises probably hoped that the presence of Lutheran theologians would weaken their opponents' position and hasten the end of the colloquy. Andreae and three others arrived shortly after the colloquy had ended, but his trip to Paris and the conversations he had with religious and political leaders there afforded him exposure to the problems of the Reformation in France.

One of Andreae's companions on this trip, Jakob Beurlin, the chancellor of the University of Tuebingen, died while they were in France. Christoph appointed Andreae to the vacant post of chancellor and made him at the same time professor of theology. After nine years as superintendent and pastor in Goeppingen, he moved to Tuebingen to assume new duties. Students heard him lecture on the New Testament and systematic theology, and he also taught homiletics.

By bestowing on Andreae the variety of assignments and duties which came to him before he was even 35 years old, Duke Christoph demonstrated his great confidence in the judgment and capability of the smithy's son who would not have gone on to university study had not Christoph's father been willing to subsidize his education. That investment was rewarded with loyal service because Andreae stood ready to provide it and because Christoph regarded him highly enough to command and use it.

A Mission to Reconcile

The year before Andreae came to Goeppingen the Truce of Passau established the temporary legality of the Lutheran confession in the Holy Roman Empire. In 1555 that legal, though inferior, status was confirmed for those who subscribed to the Augsburg Confession in the Religious Peace of Augsburg. But Roman Catholic pressure for the suppression of the Evangelicals did not vanish just because the new emperor, Ferdinand I, abrogated the Edict of Worms and abandoned the plans of his brother for the military eradication of all opposition to pope and emperor. In the face of that political pressure from churchmen and princes in the German papal party, the Evangelical princes felt compelled to organize themselves. But the creation of a common Evangelical front was frustrated by doctrinal debates among the theologians. In the wake of the Smalcaldic War disputes broke out among the Lutheran churchmen over a number of serious issues, and ecclesiastical counselors in some states had very different advice for their princes than did their counterparts in other states concerning the propriety of such a common Evangelical front.

Christoph was not only concerned about the organization and centralization of the church of Wuerttemberg; he also assumed a position of leadership among the second generation of Evangelical princes. He was anxious to unify and consolidate Evangelical political power for the security of the churches of the Augsburg Confession. That consolidation demanded harmony within the Evangelical camp. As Christoph began his efforts toward concord in the mid-1550s, he found a willing tool in Jacob Andreae. For Andreae was by disposition as well as assignment a searcher for peace and a seeker after harmony.

His own attempt to find a mediating position in the first and most devastating controversy among the reformers of the 16th century illustrates his early irenic stance and concern. The doctrine of the Lord's Supper was the occasion for a bitter dispute between Zwingli and Luther; differences over that doctrine opened up a breach between some of Melanchthon's disciples and other Lutherans during the years when Andreae was formulating his plan for Lutheran concord. In the early 1550s Lutherans pointed out that the teachings of John Calvin, then rising to European prominence as an Evangelical theologian, on the Sacrament of the Altar were closer to Zwingli's than to Luther's, and their charges opened up another phase of the Sacramentarian controversy. Into this arena Andreae climbed with his first attempt at creating concord. In 1557 he published his first book, a brief one entitled *A Short and Simple Statement Concerning the Lord's Supper and How an Ordinary Christian Should Conduct Himself in the Long and Drawn-out Controversy Which Has Arisen over It.*[3] In this book he attempted to formulate the doctrine of the Lord's Supper in a Lutheran way but also tried to avoid offending the Swiss, or at least the Genevans. The book brought cries of outrage and condemnation from at least one Gnesio-Lutheran, Nikolaus von Amsdorf, and did not produce the settlement of the issue for which Andreae had hoped.

In spite of a correspondence between Andreae and Calvin, in which they both demonstrated mutual respect and conciliatory restraint, Calvin remained disappointed with Andreae's basic Lutheran stance on the questions that divided them. Calvin's colleagues from Geneva, William Farel and Theodore Beza, did come to Goeppingen in May 1557 while on a trip through the empire to arouse Evangelical support for the French

Protestants, who were under increasing pressure from King Henry III. During their visit they made important concessions as they joined Andreae in setting down a statement that was to be used as the basis for a colloquy on the Lord's Supper between their party and the German theologians of the Augsburg Confession. But Bullinger, Zwingli's successor in Zurich, denounced Andreae, and the strongly Lutheran stance of the German Evangelical princes on the Lord's Supper discouraged further efforts along these lines. Although Andreae still attempted to present formulations of the doctrine of the Lord's Supper which would be acceptable to Calvinists in 1559 and 1560,[4] this effort at concord aroused opposition from both sides and served only to make some Lutherans suspicious of the young churchman from Goeppingen.

Christoph was not disturbed, however, and involved Andreae in his own efforts to promote Lutheran unity. Andreae was with him at the Diet of Regensburg in early 1557 as he promoted his plans for an Evangelical coalition, and the duke asked the advice of Andreae and others on his ecclesiastical staff in regard to moving ahead with the implementation of these plans. When representatives of the Roman Catholic and the Evangelical parties met at Worms in the summer of 1557 to discuss the issues that divided them, Andreae was nominated by Christoph as one of the Evangelical notaries for the colloquy, and he served in that capacity throughout the short-lived conversations. The colloquy broke up because the Gnesio-Lutheran representatives insisted upon the condemnation of a series of errors, some of which they alleged were held by other Evangelical members of the colloquy panel. As in the previous year, during the visitation of Baden-Durlach, Andreae saw at Worms the deeply felt divisions of northern German Lutheranism embarrass his position in front of the Roman opposition. This must have heightened his sense of concern over the disputes within the churches of the Augsburg Confession.

Christoph used Andreae for several other reconciling missions during the early 1560s. In 1562 ducal Saxony, the citadel of Gnesio-Lutheranism, was torn apart by a debate between two of the members of the theological faculty at the University of Jena, Matthias Flacius Illyricus and Viktorin Strigel. Their debate over the freedom of the will and original sin had alienated Strigel from most of the clergymen of the land. However, Duke John Frederick the Middler had become impatient with Flacius and had favored Strigel in the settlement of their dispute.

John Frederick asked Christoph to send theologians to help him restore theological solidarity to his church, and Christoph obliged by sending Andreae and a colleague, Christoph Binder, the superintendent of Nuertingen. They arrived in Weimar in April 1562, conducted conversations with Strigel and his supporters, and concluded that Strigel was not guilty of the synergism of which he had been accused. Andreae was disappointed by the reoccurrence of synergistic expressions in Strigel's writings during the course of the next year.

In the church of Strassburg a serious dispute broke out about the same time as the Strigel-Flacius controversy in ducal Saxony. Johann Marbach, exponent of a strict Lutheran position, disagreed on a number of points with the heirs of the era in which Martin Bucer had led the reform movement in Strassburg. The mediating Bucer had tried to find middle ground on which Wittenbergers and Zurichers could meet, and the humanistic educator Johann Sturm, who remained in the city after the Interim had driven Bucer to England, tried to continue to foster the spirit of the early Strassburg reformation after Marbach rose to prominence in the city. Among Sturm's supporters was Hieronymus Zanchi, professor of Old Testament at the Strassburg Academy. Zanchi and Marbach disagreed on the Lord's Supper and on the doctrine of predestination, and Zanchi asked for a colloquy in which he could obtain a hearing before theologians from outside Strassburg. Andreae joined one theologian from the Palatinate-Zweibruecken and two from Basel as the panel which sought a solution to the Strassburg dispute. The solution was not to be found, however, for Zanchi and Marbach could not overcome their differences.

Exactly a year later, in April 1564, Andreae again had to deal with the differences between Reformed and Lutheran theologians on the Lord's Supper in a colloquium, this time between the theologians of Wuerttemberg and those of the Palatinate. In 1563 Elector Frederick III of the Palatinate turned his land, only recently reformed, from its initial Lutheran position toward that of Calvin. With the publication of the Heidelberg Catechism in 1563 a new crisis of unity appeared, and Duke Christoph called his own theologians together—Andreae, of course, among them—in September to study the catechism and comment on its implications for German Evangelical unity. The following spring Andreae and his colleagues met with the theologians of the Palatinate at Maulbronn, but their discussions only highlighted the differences

17

between them. The representatives of Elector Frederick criticized the Wuerttembergers' understanding of the ubiquity of Christ as unscriptural. Andreae must have left the meeting with a greater concern than ever for reversing the trend toward disagreement and for establishing a firm basis for Evangelical unity.

The concern of Andreae and his prince, Duke Christoph, for the unity of the church found opportunity for action five years later when Duke Julius of Braunschweig-Wolfenbuettel requested help from Wuerttemberg in the Evangelical reorganization of the church in his lands. At that time Andreae was finally able to initiate the first of his programs for ending the discord which wracked the churches of his confession.

Controversies and Attempts at Conciliation

The world into which Jakob Andreae was born was changing rapidly, more rapidly perhaps than the European world had changed for centuries. New political forces were diminishing the power of medieval custom and right and were concentrating powers in the hands of territorial princes and kings. New legal forms were altering social and economic relationships. Commerce and industry were expanding at the beginning of the 16th century in the Holy Roman Empire, and new methods were being applied to various aspects of economic life. The educational system was not the same as it had been a century earlier, for humanists were teaching alongside scholastics at the university and in the academy.

An integral part of the culture's transformation centered in the reformation of its religious life and thought. A decade before Andreae's birth Martin Luther had aroused hopes and antagonisms with his proclamation of his understanding of the Christian Gospel, and Andreae's life and lifework were determined in large part by Luther's proclamation and life.

The Smalcaldic War

The emperor of the Holy Roman Empire, Charles V, had pledged his government at Worms in 1521 to the eradication of Luther's Gospel. A series of events and factors prevented the emperor from proceeding with plans to carry out the Edict of Worms until Andreae was at the university, but in 1547 it appeared that the cause of the Evangelical Reformation might well be overcome and eradicated by its enemies.

Charles V went to war against his two leading antagonists among the Evangelical princes, Elector John Frederick of Saxony and Landgrave Philip of Hesse, in the summer of 1546.[5] The two were leaders of the Smalcaldic League, a group of Evangelical princes and cities formed in 1532 to oppose efforts of the imperial government to eradicate Lutheran "heresy." They had both broken imperial law, Philip by becoming a bigamist and John Frederick by seizing the bishopric of Naumburg-Zeitz and the lands of the canons of Wurzen by force. These and other offenses of the two princes gave Charles the pretext he needed to separate his crusade against them from the religious issue, which might have won them additional princely support.

One of the Evangelical princes whom Charles enticed away from the Evangelical cause during the Smalcaldic War was Moritz, duke of Saxony. Moritz, nephew and successor of the arch-Roman Catholic Duke George, had followed his father and immediate predecessor, Duke Heinrich, into the Evangelical faith. But he also became a friend of Charles V and particularly of Charles' brother Ferdinand, archduke of Austria and king of Bohemia. Moritz was drawn into cooperating with the emperor. He invaded the lands of his cousin John Frederick when the elector led the Evangelical army south toward the Austrian lands of the Hapsburgs Charles V and Ferdinand. John Frederick and Philip pulled back before they had defeated the imperial forces so that John Frederick might free his lands from the forces of his cousin Moritz, who had occupied electoral Saxony. By late winter 1547 John Frederick had pushed Moritz out of electoral Saxony and had occupied most of Moritz's own territory. But Charles V and Ferdinand came to the rescue of their Evangelical ally. On April 24, 1547, the Spanish and German troops of the emperor caught the forces of John Frederick at Muehlberg on the Elbe, and in a day-long battle the imperial army defeated the Evangelicals. John Frederick and Philip were taken prisoner. On May 19 John Frederick signed the Wittenberg Capitulation, which gave Moritz his title as elector and much of his land. His sons, however, were made dukes of Saxony in Thuringia, the western part of his territory.

The Interims and the Adiaphoristic Controversy

Charles followed up his victory on the field with plans for consolidating his hold over the Holy Roman Empire. At the diet at Augsburg which began the next September he appointed a commission to prepare regulations for the religious life of the empire for the interim before the Council of Trent would make final disposition of the problems besetting 16th-century Christendom. The commission appointed a subcommittee of three: two Erasmian Roman Catholics, Michael Helding, suffragan bishop of Mainz, and Julius von Pflug, newly installed bishop of Naumburg-Zeitz; and the Evangelical court preacher of Elector Joachim II of Brandenburg, Johann Agricola (see pp. 31—32).[6]

Two Spanish theologians from Charles' retinue and his brother Ferdinand's court preacher also took part in the composition of the *Declaration on Religion* which the committee presented to Charles. Known popularly as the Augsburg Interim, it conceded to Evangelicals who sought permission the right to distribute Communion in both kinds and the right of priests to marry. However, it also imposed Roman dogma upon them. The Interim linked justification to the gift of *caritas*, and thus to the practice of good works. It restored the power of papal bishops and the authority of the pope. It reestablished all seven medieval sacraments. It defended the medieval practice of the Mass and insisted that the Evangelicals use its traditional form and trappings as well as the sacramentals which involved various areas of church life. The Interim, if enforced, spelled the end of Lutheranism.

The Interim was proclaimed May 15, 1548, and Charles V proceeded forthwith to enforce it in Evangelical lands and cities where he could.[7] Wuerttemberg was occupied by Spanish troops, as were several southern Evangelical cities. Various degrees of compliance were obtained in various places. Only two Evangelical pastors in all Wuerttemberg actually consented to remain in their congregations and conduct their ministries according to the Augsburg Interim.[8]

In print the opposition to the Augsburg Interim began almost immediately after its publication. Several Lutheran writers issued strong denunciations of the Interim, especially of its Evangelical co-author Agricola, and forcefully rejected any compromise with the emperor and the Roman party. Others, among them Luther's close friend Philip Melanchthon, expressed themselves more cautiously. For the outcome of the Smalcaldic War had placed Melanchthon and some of his Saxon colleagues in a peculiar situation, in many ways more difficult than that of those who had been driven form their pastorates. For Melanchthon and the entire Wittenberg University faculty lived in the area which now owed allegiance to the new elector of Saxony, Moritz. Moritz found himself caught in a vise. On the one hand, he felt pressure from his Hapsburg friends, who were not about to keep their oral promise, made before the war, that Moritz would not have to change his faith. On the other hand, he felt pressure from his estates and subjects, who were uncompromisingly Lutheran in spirit and doctrine. Moritz tried to convince the Saxons that the return of Spanish troops to Saxon soil was a genuine threat at the same time he was doing his best to convince Charles that he was trying to comply with the Augsburg Interim, for in 1548 he still believed that his hold on his electorate and his new lands was no stronger than his ability to keep the emperor's favor.

Moritz's theologians issued a series of memoranda on the Interim, counseling rejection but allowing that certain compromises could be made concerning adiaphora. When Moritz returned from the imperial diet in Augsburg in early summer 1548, he inaugurated a series of consultations in which his theologians were led and badgered by his secular advisers into forging a compromise settlement. This compromise, called the Leipzig Interim, was adopted by the Saxon estates assembled at Leipzig in late December 1548.

The Leipzig Interim satisfied no one in trying to placate the emperor while trying to preserve the heart of Lutheran doctrine. The basic principle of the Leipzig Interim was concession on indifferent matters and retention of the Evangelical understanding of justification.[9]

The Leipzig Interim was viewed by its authors as a document of compromise chiefly in its concessions in what they considered adiaphora. The Interim accepted confirmation (holding out hope it could be transformed from a spectacle into an examination of faith), private confession before Communion, and extreme unction practiced according to apostolic usage. It restored much of the Latin rite of the Roman Mass as well as the traditional vestments, bells, lamps, vessels—the ceremonial of the old worship service. Moritz's theologians also conceded the restoration of the canonical hours and services in memory of the dead. They planned for the reintroduction of many of the old festival celebrations, including Corpus Christi and Marian holidays. According to this second Interim, meat would not be eaten on Fridays and Saturdays in Saxony, in obedience to the civil ordinances of the empire. Perhaps the most difficult part of the new formula to compose and to sell to the estates was that which dealt with the right of the bishops to ordain. The Saxon bishops were all papal appointees after the Smalcaldic War, but the Saxon theologians were willing to acknowledge their right to ordain all pastors if the bishops did not persecute the Gospel and if they strove for good order in the church. Candidates for ordination had to be presented to the bishop by the patron of the congregation, a stipulation that insured control by Evangelical lords over the churches in their lands.

The Leipzig Interim was forged by men of good will and genuine concern, but they were men of a different spirit and perhaps of less common sense than those who quickly rose up to oppose them. For example, one of those who framed the Leipzig Interim, Prince Georg of Anhalt, had always favored conservative liturgical practices; what to others were papalist trappings had always been to him proper Christian forms. Johann Pfeffinger, pastor and professor in Leipzig, had served Moritz for the better part of a decade as an ecclesiastical counselor, as had others who participated in the composition of the Leipzig Interim. These men knew Moritz had established and supported the Evangelical faith in his lands, and they were willing to help him preserve as much of that faith as possible by compromising, hoping thereby to prevent an imperial invasion of Saxony.

Melanchthon was drawn to his new elector in part because Moritz defended and supported his university and also was actively trying to protect his leading theologian from the wrath of Charles V. He was genuinely concerned about the threat of Spanish troops and the religious suppression and persecution their renewed presence in Saxony would bring. In addition, he believed that the stars foretold an early death for Charles V; buying a little time through compromise would be worthwhile since a new emperor would soon mount the throne. Furthermore, concessions in adiaphora had never been offensive to him. He therefore acceded to the desires of his prince—not without misgivings but without rancor or an extended rear-guard retreat filled with excuses. Melanchthon was willing to compromise appearances for the sake of peace for his prince, his university, his fellow Saxons. He did not survey the larger implications, beyond peace at that time and in his land, as did a group of Luther's associates who gathered in the city of Magdeburg in 1548 and 1549. The group included Nikolaus von Amsdorf, Matthias Flacius Illyricus, Nikolaus Gallus and others. As professor at Wittenberg and confidant to the new elector of Saxony, Melanchthon's options were more limited than were those of an exiled bishop like Amsdorf or a student on the run like Flacius in the outlawed city of Magdeburg.[10]

Magdeburg was theoretically subject in the secular as well as the ecclesiastical realm to the archbishop of Magdeburg, but the desire of its citizens to be free of his control had coincided with the sincere conviction wrought in their hearts concerning religious reformation by its ecclesiastical superintendent Amsdorf and others in the 1520s. In 1548 the city became a haven for those who opposed the Augsburg Interim. The city had held out against Charles V after the Smalcaldic War when

Moritz was assigned to reduce it. Under the leadership of Amsdorf and Flacius, the Gnesio-Lutheran party developed there in the period before the besieged city surrendered to Moritz in 1551.

As two parties, Anglicans and Puritans, arose in England during its Reformation, so circumstances in Saxony led to the development of two groups within its young Lutheran church. One group favored—from the late medieval perspective—a relatively more conservative Reformation; the other group wanted to take Luther's insights in their full radicality, at times expressing them in an even more radical fashion than Luther himself had. The conservatives have been named the Philippists because of their allegiance to their preceptor, Melanchthon; and the radicals, often called the Flacianists, are better designated the Gnesio-Lutherans (since not all Gnesio-Lutherans followed Flacius blindly but some fought bitterly with him).

The differing attitudes toward the Reformation which finally became concrete in the somewhat loosely associated groups called Philippists and Gnesio-Lutherans did not begin only after or because of the crisis caused by the Smalcaldic War. Nor was it inevitable that Luther's death would initiate a series of squabbles over the correct definition of his message. But questions had been raised between his closest friends during his lifetime over several issues that would become centers of controversy within Lutheranism in the three decades following his death. These included the necessity of good works for eternal life, the role of the human will in conversion and the Christian life, and the real presence of Christ in the Lord's Supper.[11] These questions were raised again by various events connected with the Interims, and they were raised in an atmosphere which was being poisoned by political considerations and personal recriminations arising from differing views of what was best for the Evangelical church of Saxony. From Magdeburg came charges that Moritz of Saxony was a newborn Antiochus Epiphanes and that his theologians had sold out to the Antichrist of Rome. Such criticism threatened to upset Moritz's precarious hold on his lands, both new and old, since his people were solidly Evangelical. From Wittenberg and Leipzig came countercharges that the men of Magdeburg were rebels and riffraff, outlaws and schismatics. The issue of compromise with the Roman Church at points the electoral Saxons considered adiaphora became the focal point for a rivalry which grew up between friends, between two groups of the students of Luther and Melanchthon. The political necessities of the situations of men on each side provided the spark for what developed into a quarter century of intense and sometimes bitter exchanges of charges and countercharges.

The Gnesio-Lutheran attack on the Leipzig Interim poured forth in the course of 1549 and 1550 from the presses of Magdeburg, practically the only place in the empire where tracts against either Interim could be published. The Magdeburgers objected to the presuppositions and judgments concerning adiaphora which the Wittenbergers and Leipzigers had had to make in forging the Leipzig Interim. In a tract by Amsdorf, Flacius, and Gallus they set down their basic principle: "In a case where confession of the faith is demanded, where ceremonies or adiaphora are commanded as necessary, where offense may be given, adiaphora do not remain adiaphora or indifferent but become matters of moral precept, in which God must be obeyed." Amsdorf and Flacius could not have cared less about how theologians might explain away their concessions to Rome. They were concerned about the effect of these concessions on the average Saxon parishioner. The Interimists were declaring that it was better to bring back the surplice, light an almost forgotten candle, sing a Latin verse, and still preach the Gospel, than it would be to have Spanish troops and papal priests marching into Saxony. Amsdorf and company were really no more secure in the embattled city of Magdeburg, but they felt safer or chose to ignore the imperial threat and to concentrate on the pastoral needs of that parishioner. They replied to the electoral Saxon theologians that the average parishioner saw as much as he heard in worship. If he saw the surplice and the candle, he would believe that the Wittenbergers who had reintroduced these papalist practices had returned to the message of the old days as well. He would not hear the Gospel because the reminders of Rome would seem to indicate that Luther's successors had forgotten it. The exiled pastors at Magdeburg had lived their ministries among people for whom words were less important than symbols. As a professor Melanchthon was at a disadvantage when it came to reading the popular mind. His colleagues and he had responded to other pressures and a somewhat different concern.

The controversy over the Interims became unnecessary after the Truce of Passau in 1552 and the Religious Peace of Augsburg in 1555. The Interims were dead. However, the controversy had burned too hotly for it to be put out at once. The Gnesio-Lutherans insisted that the Philippists repent publicly for their composition and defense of the Leipzig Interim.

Although Melanchthon did admit that he had taken the wrong stand,[12] he and his followers refused to submit to the kind of public penance Flacius and his friends insisted upon. So the two parties continued to exchange verbal and printed blasts on the subject of the Interim throughout the 1550s. They also found other issues over which to dispute.

The Majoristic Controversy

Among those Wittenbergers who attacked the Magdeburgers in the debate over the Leipzig Interim were Georg Major and Johann Bugenhagen. In late 1551 Amsdorf replied to the accusations of these two former friends of his in a fiery little piece entitled *That Dr. Pomer and Dr. Major Along with Their Adiaphorists Have Caused Offense and Schism and Have Done the Churches of Christ Insurmountable Harm.*[13] Amsdorf made a special point of the omission of the words *sola fide* in the Leipzig Interim; and he criticized those who taught that good works are necessary for salvation, as the Interim did. Major felt constrained to defend his position. He emphasized his own insistence on justification through faith alone but also stated:

> This I confess; I have previously taught and still teach and want to
> teach my whole life, that good works are necessary to salvation, and I
> say openly and with clear and plain words, that no one will be saved
> through evil works and no one will be saved without good works, and
> I further say whoever teaches otherwise, even an angel from heaven,
> is accursed.[14]

Amsdorf replied immediately with more heat than light. He was joined by others of the Gnesio-Lutheran party, who accused Major of returning to "papist, Pelagian" works-righteousness. Major denied that and insisted that he had always taught that salvation is given only by God's grace through faith in Christ. But he also insisted that faith produces works, that faith is always joined to new obedience. Therefore the works of the Christian, he maintained, are a necessary part of his salvation.

Major was echoing Melanchthon's concern for Christian ethics and was well aware of the danger of antinomianism in the Evangelical camp. As a member of the Saxon consistory he was faced directly with problems of moral breakdown in a Christian state. Amsdorf, on the other hand, could never forget that the papal supporters who had tried to eradicate the infant Evangelical movement in Magdeburg used the concept of the necessity of good works for salvation as a weapon against the preaching of Luther's doctrines. Amsdorf was convinced that Evangelical laymen only a generation away from late medieval papalism could understand words like "good works are necessary for salvation" in only one way. He was extremely sensitive to the problem of misrepresenting the fruits of faith as the seed of faith, whereas Major was reacting to those who felt that they did not need to do good works since they had faith. Other Gnesio-Lutherans shared his concern. Although the pressure of attack on Major was diverted temporarily to his friend Justus Menius,[15] Flacius and his colleagues continued to treat Major's proposition as a serious threat to Luther's understanding of the Gospel until Major's death.

One phase of the Gnesio-Lutheran reaction to Major caused a minor controversy itself. Amsdorf had insited on the necessity of good works in Christian living, as a result of faith, throughout his attack on the concept of their necessity for salvation. However, in an effort to clarify his concern over Major's proposition, he formulated one of his own: "Good works are harmful for salvation." He indicated in a tract on his proposition that good works are harmful when one trusts in them for salvation.[16] Most theologians on both sides of the Majoristic controversy knew what he meant and ignored him. Some Philippists could not help but throw the charge of antinomianism his way, in part at least because of their concern that Evangelical laymen could well get the idea that freedom from the Law, as Luther proclaimed it, meant also freedom from works. Amsdorf's error was added to the list of those which the Lutherans of the late 16th century were bound to notice and reject, but no serious dispute grew up around his proposition.

Major found almost no supporters for his proposition, and the matter would have sunk from public view had he been able to extricate himself more convincingly from his unfortunate formulation. But without public repentance the Gnesio-Lutherans could not be satisfied that the proposition had properly been removed from Lutheran theological circles, and so the issue lingered in the public exchanges between Gnesio-Lutherans and Philippists until the Formula of Concord ended the debate.

The Synergistic Controversies

Johann Pfeffinger, superintendent and professor in Leipzig, like many Philippists, had studied at Wittenberg in the 1520s and was a loyal friend of Melanchthon. He served Moritz as pastor, professor, and ecclesiastical adviser from the duke's accession in 1541. He helped compose and defend the Leipzig Interim. Therefore when he suggested in public disputation in 1555 that man is able with his own natural powers to assent to the Word, to grasp the promise, and not to resist the Holy Spirit, Gnesio-Lutherans found it impossible not to suspect that he was denying the sole efficacy of God's grace. Strangely enough, they waited three years before attacking his view.

As a student of Melanchthon's, Pfeffinger had been taught that the human will, along with the Word and the Holy Spirit, is the third factor in conversion.[17] The humanists of the Philippist school wrestled with the psychological aspects of the relationship between God and man in a way the Gnesio-Lutherans did not. Pfeffinger was struggling with the problems of determinism and human reaction to God's grace when he wrote: "We attribute some cooperation to our will, [but] this sort of assent and grasping takes absolutely nothing at all away from the aid of the Holy Spirit." Yet he qualified and obscured his insistence on the primacy of the Holy Spirit by adding that the "Holy Spirit is received in this way by those who seek [Him], that is, by those who do not spurn or reject Him, but who seek His aid with groaning."[18]

Amsdorf criticized Pfeffinger for this position in 1558, at the same time that Flacius and Johann Stolz, court preacher for the dukes of Saxony, published their critiques of Pfeffinger's theses.[19] Pfeffinger replied, but he was never able to make it clear whether the human will could cooperate with God's grace before or only after the Holy Spirit moved that will. The controversy moved quite quickly beyond Pfeffinger at Leipzig into ducal Saxony itself.

The sons of John Frederick, as dukes of the Thuringian corner of their father's former domains, had begun a new university at Jena to replace Wittenberg, which had fallen to Moritz's control in 1547. The University of Jena, which received its imperial charter in 1558, was unavoidably something of a filial institution of Wittenberg, for the trained academics of Saxony had come in large part from the school of Melanchthon and Luther. Jena's first professor of theology, Viktorin Strigel, was recommended by Melanchthon for his position. Only 24 years old when he arrived in Jena in 1548, the brilliant Strigel became something of a *Wunderkind* in ducal Saxon ecclesiastical life. He felt his position severely threatened when in 1557 Flacius, four years his elder, joined the theological faculty at Jena. He also must have resented what he

28

regarded as Flacius' rude treatment of their common mentor Melanchthon, for Strigel, though he served dukes generally sympathetic to the Gnesio-Lutheran position, had remained on good terms with Melanchthon and still shared views and concerns similar to his preceptor's.

For three years the two jockeyed for position within the ducal Saxon church. Their antagonism burst into the open when Duke John Frederick the Middler determined in 1557 to further Lutheran unity by sponsoring the composition of a *Book of Confutation*. The *Book* was to condemn clearly and definitively the errors which concerned the Gnesio-Lutherans. The duke asked Strigel and two of his friends to work on this *Book,* but they refused unless Amsdorf and Flacius would be completely excluded from any part in the project. The duke consented to this condition. The three proceeded to formulate a rough draft, which they offered to the duke in early 1558, repeating their expressed stipulation that Amsdorf and Flacius not be allowed to change a word.

Strigel and his friends hardly recognized their text when Flacius and a group of others got done with their revisions. This affront to Strigel's group only heightened the antagonism and friction within the ducal Saxon church. Ducal intervention in the feud set the scene for open confrontation between Strigel and Flacius. Strigel had refused to subscribe to the *Book of Confutation* as revised by Flacius on the basis of his rejection of a few of its statements. He hoped to defeat Flacius and regain his leading position in the church of ducal Saxony by defending the stance he had held since Melanchthon had instructed him 15 years earlier.

Strigel's resistance to the duke's command that all clergy subscribe to the *Book of Confutation* angered John Frederick the Middler, and Strigel was arrested and imprisoned in the spring of 1559. After enforced meditation upon the *Book's* position in two ducal castles, Strigel still could not formulate his position, particularly on the role of the human will in conversion, to the satisfaction of the duke's clerical advisers. But pressure from the emperor and other Evangelical princes, together with John Frederick's own concern for pure doctrine and his weariness with the wrangle among his theologians, made the duke press for settlement. He rejected Strigel's suggestion for a synod of all Lutheran churches and opted for Flacius' proposal for a disputation between himself and Strigel.

The participants in this Weimar disputation did not discuss all the issues put before them; the duke became impatient with the proceedings and placed the disputation in permanent recess after 13 sessions. Free will and its role in man's conversion were the central issue during the disputation, and in the context of the discussion of this issue a new controversy was born. Flacius wanted to view man Biblically; Strigel wanted to take Aristotelian anthropology seriously as a framework for Biblical anthropology. Flacius blundered onto Strigel's field of battle, adopted his terminology, and countered Strigel's claim that original sin was an accident in man with the assertion that man's very substance since the fall is original sin. Flacius was charged with Manichaeism; this may have contributed to John Frederick's growing disillusion with him.

Strigel defined man's will after the fall as a neutral, unbound active force; that was for him not so much a theological as a philosophical premise. Flacius believed the will is bound and unable in any way to turn to God; he was thinking only theologically. Strigel argued that man remains God's creature and that his will retains its mode of acting in spite of sin, which is only an accidental property of man's substance. The latter is good because it was created in the image of God. Flacius asserted that original sin is not merely accidental but has permeated and perverted the whole substance of man, who as a result of the fall is shaped essentially in the image of Satan, not in the image of God. Flacius taught this because he felt that any other appraisal of man did not take seriously his total depravity.[20]

Throughout the rest of his life, at great personal cost, Flacius developed and maintained the basic position he had set forth at the Weimar Disputation. Duke John Frederick the Middler found that Flacius and his followers were increasingly difficult to keep in line, so in the winter of 1561 the duke purged the Flacianists on the theological faculty. After he presented his anthropology and his view of original sin as the substance of man in his *Key to the Sacred Scriptures* in 1567, Flacius found few friends even among the Gnesio-Lutherans. Johann Wigand and Tilemann Hesshus in particular criticized his position in print; only a few younger Lutheran pastors tried to defend him and carried on his argument after he died.

Andreae became directly involved with both sides in the synergistic controversy. In April 1562 Duke Christoph sent him and Christoph Binder to Weimar at the request of Duke John Frederick the Middler, who appealed to Wuerttemberg for help in settling the Strigel crisis after Flacius had been exiled. Andreae and Binder met with Strigel, formulated a "Declaration" which Strigel could sign, and urged that it be a new standard for belief in ducal Saxony. In its first section Strigel confessed that man is indeed corrupt and impotent until the Holy Spirit moves him to trust in God. In the second section he asserted that man had a *modus agendi*, a capacity or aptitude which plays a role in conversion. Strigel was concerned that man's psychological functions not be ignored in the discussion of conversion, but he was unable or unwilling to refine his statement in a way that ruled out any human contribution to one's own conversion. This second portion of the "Declaration of Viktorin" aroused instant hostility among the clergy of ducal Saxony, and many of them followed Flacius and Wigand into exile over the course of the next year, undoubtedly filled with some resentment toward Andreae, who had arranged the settlement. Later Andreae expressed his disillusionment with Strigel's position as it was expressed in comments on Psalms 95 and 119, written in 1563. Andreae and Binder viewed these comments as synergistic and felt that they had been deceived by Strigel. But neither side pursued the matter in public debate.

Andreae also discussed anthropology with Flacius in the subsequent decade. They met in 1567 in Strassburg and again in 1571 to attempt to reach common ground in the definition of original sin. Their efforts ended in an exchange of somewhat bitter polemic in 1573 and 1574. Andreae found common ground with other Gnesio-Lutherans in combating Flacius' concept of original sin and his anthropological terminology, and this common ground helped lay the foundation for the structure of harmony which Wuerttembergers and Lower Saxons would build together.

Controversies over Law and Gospel

Related to the disputes between Philippists and Gnesio-Lutherans which have been discussed above are the several disputes over Law and Gospel among Luther's heirs. The first such debate, the only one in which a genuinely "antinomian" position was defended, actually predates the Philippist vs. Gnesio-Lutheran split. It involved Luther himself on the one side against Johann Agricola, one of his earliest students and followers. After nearly 10 years at Wittenberg, Agricola moved to Eisleben to become first a rector of the local school and then a pastor. In early 1526 Melanchthon assumed a lectureship in theology at Wittenberg which Agricola had wanted for himself, and from that point Agricola seems to have felt estranged from the Wittenbergers. However, when he criticized Melanchthon's treatment of the Law in the church in the Saxon Visitation Articles of 1527, he was only developing a line of thought found in earlier writings.[21] With Luther, Agricola reacted against the legalism and works-righteousness of popular late medieval belief, but he went beyond Luther to ban the Law from the life of the Christian. He taught that the Gospel reveals the wrath of God and produces contrition alongside its effecting the forgiveness of sins. Christ ended the reign of the Law, which God had designed for the Jews, Agricola believed, and thus in the life of the Christian only the Gospel can be preached. Implicit in his understanding of the Law's relation to the Christian life was his understanding of sin, which he limited to a certain extent only to sin against the First Commandment, unbelief. In reaction to the medieval stress on actual, committed sins, he almost ignored these sins and thus believed that man becomes right with God without any preaching of the Law directed against sins. The Gospel serves to alert man to his need for salvation in Agricola's system.

Luther did not take seriously the rift between his two friends, Melanchthon and Agricola, until Agricola moved back to Wittenberg in 1537. In Wittenberg Agricola attacked the use of the Law in the church and let it be known that he believed Luther had abandoned his original Gospel. Tensions grew between the two throughout 1537, even though Agricola was still involved in university instruction in theology. Luther felt betrayed by his friend and disciple, but the two managed a reconciliation. However, their dispute simmered and then broke out again in open, formal disputation within the university structure in early 1539. Although Luther had only slowly come to oppose Agricola's teaching, once angered at his former student, he pushed for condemnation of his views. With support from other longtime friends in Wittenberg, he moved to suspend Agricola's right to teach at the university, for he had come to believe that Agricola's position perverted the Gospel as he had taught it. Elector John Frederick the Elder intervened in the matter in 1540 and forbade Agricola to leave Wittenberg until the case had been settled. Agricola, in fear and resentment, fled Wittenberg and became court preacher at Berlin for Elector Joachim II of Brandenburg. In that capacity he played his strange role in the writing of the Augsburg Interim.

The later "antinomian" disputes, which did feature Gnesio-

32

Lutherans and Philippists, grew out of a concern similar to that of Agricola's, out of a reaction against works-righteousness and the use of the Law as at least a partial means of effecting one's own salvation. But no one in the two later antinomian disputes actually wanted to assign the Law no role in the proclamation of the church and the life of the Christian. Both of these later "antinomian" disputes arose out of the Majoristic controversy over the proposition: "Good works are necessary for salvation."

The first controversy did not really flare into public print until at the Altenburg Colloquy in 1568 the Philippist representatives from electoral Saxony accused one Gnesio-Lutheran, Anton Otto, of crass antinomianism. But no extended public discussion even resulted from that false accusation. The dispute in which Otto had played a small role over a decade earlier arose out of the Eisenach Synod of 1556. That synod had been called to decide the fate of Justus Menius, who had been accused of Majorism. Among its decisions was one which declared: "Good works are necessary for salvation theoretically in the doctrine of the Law." That formulation was attacked by Amsdorf, by Otto, pastor in Nordhausen, and particularly by Andreas Poach, pastor in Erfurt. Flacius and Wigand dealt with Amsdorf's objections; Joachim Moerlin of Braunschweig carried on the dispute with Poach—the controversy pitted Gnesio-Lutheran against Gnesio-Lutheran. Amsdorf, Otto, and Poach were concerned that even this formulation would encourage reliance on one's own works for salvation. Flacius and Moerlin argued that the Law is the basis of judgment only if its demands are indeed the requirement for life as God originally created it for man.[22]

More public and more serious was the controversy between two of Agricola's colleagues in Brandenburg in the late 1550s and early 1560s. Andreas Musculus had studied at Wittenberg in the late 1530s and had become a friend of Agricola and a disciple of Luther before accepting a call to Frankfurt an der Oder as a pastor and professor in 1540. In 1557 Melanchthon's disciple Abdias (Gottschalk) Praetorius became professor of Hebrew at Frankfurt. Agricola and then Musculus took exception to Praetorius' use of the proposition: "Good works are necessary," and fought a five-year running battle in print, in preaching, and in the lecture hall. Students in Frankfurt generally sided with Praetorius, the clergy in Brandenburg was divided, and Elector Joachim tried a number of times to reconcile his quarreling professors. Although he supported Musculus' position, he was never alienated from Praetorius and used him as a counselor and legate until Praetorius finally moved to Wittenberg in 1563.[23]

Musculus taught that good works are produced freely through the Holy Spirit in the Christian life; Praetorius said that good works are a necessary part of the Christian life. Musculus knew what this position could mean in Brandenburg less than a generation after the Evangelical faith had become established. He was convinced that many laymen would interpret the necessity of good works as a soteriological statement and revert or retrench to their old belief that doing good works saves. Praetorius shared the concern of his Philippist colleagues against antinomianism. He knew that laymen could interpret Luther's message of freedom from the Law as freedom from good works. Mixed in with court intrigue and personality clashes as this controversy was, it is no wonder that its debate was particularly bitter. Both sides were trying to make a point that was important for the church in Brandenburg. Both sides misstated their own concerns and misinterpreted their opponents' concerns. Musculus won a reputation as an antinomian which even his subscription to Article VI of the Formula of Concord has not removed.

Gnesio-Lutherans and Philippists also debated, though not intensely, over the definition of the word "Gospel" in the late 1550s and early 1560s. Strigel and others who had studied under Melanchthon recognized a wider definition of "Gospel" which included the preaching of repentance. Strigel and Flacius had disagreed over this definition during their feud in ducal Saxony at the end of the 1550s, and the dispute was taken up in print by Paul Crell and Christoph Pezel among the Wittenbergers in 1570. Their position was criticized by Wigand, who agreed with Flacius that the Gospel means simply the good news of the forgiveness of sins in Jesus Christ.

The Osiandrian Controversy

The controversies discussed to this point took place in the context of the Wittenberg Reformation; that is, the disputing parties were composed largely of people who had studied at Wittenberg under Luther and Melanchthon. That was not the case with another controversy which broke out about the same time the adiaphoristic controversy arose. The Osiandrian controversy was different from those which have been discussed so far.

34

Andreas Osiander, the reformer of Nuernberg, had not attended the University of Wittenberg. Melanchthon's great-uncle Johannes Reuchlin, the great German Hebraist, had instructed Osiander at Ingolstadt, and before he arrived in Nuernberg in 1522 he had steeped himself in the mystical theology of the Kabbala and in the writings of the Italian Platonist and Hebraist Pico della Mirandola. Osiander's basic intellectual orientation was vastly different from that of the Wittenbergers. He claimed to have developed his own peculiar understanding of saving righteousness very early in his career, but his views became widely known only after he was forced into exile in Prussia when the Augsburg Interim was imposed upon Nuernberg in 1548. As an old friend of Duke Albrecht of Prussia, who shared many of his theological convictions, Osiander moved quickly over the heads of other theologians in Koenigsberg. In his inaugural disputation on April 5, 1549, he presented theses on Law and Gospel and was attacked by a Wittenberg graduate, Matthias Lauterwald. This began a feud within East Prussia which figured in the political life of the dukedom until Albrecht's death in 1568, although the controversy died down to a great extent after Osiander's death in 1552.[24]

The most prominent among the Prussian opponents of Osiander was Joachim Moerlin, a Wittenberg product who had been driven from his pastorate in Goettingen and arrived in Koenigsberg in the autumn of 1550. At first he tried to support Osiander but gradually found serious differences between his own and Osiander's theology. The important points of difference between Moerlin and Osiander centered in the latter's understanding of justification. He rejected forensic justification and taught that the believer's righteousness is the eternal righteousness of God, indwelling in him in the person of Christ. Osiander distinguished redemption or reconciliation, which took place to Christ's death 1,500 years earlier, from justification, which takes place when the eternal divine righteousness comes in the person of Christ to dwell in the believer. Other aspects of Osiander's thought also aroused suspicion, including his distinction of the inner word from the outer word and his teaching that Christ would have come to earth as the Image of God even if man had not sinned.

Although all sides in East Prussia showed a certain reluctance to engage in controversy, once the dispute had begun it was fired by polemic from almost all other Evangelical churches. Philippists and

35

Gnesio-Lutherans alike attacked Osiander and agreed that saving righteousness consists in Christ's obedience, death, and resurrection, imputed to the believer, in whom the Holy Spirit does dwell. Calvin also objected to Osiander's doctrines. Almost alone among prominent Evangelical theologians in his moderation toward Osiander was Johann Brenz of Wuerttemberg.

Melanchthon and his followers, Flacius, Amsdorf, and the other Magdeburgers and ducal Saxon theologians, Musculus in Brandenburg, and the ministeria of the Lower Saxon cities all wrote fierce criticisms of Osiander, sparked and spurred by the violence of his own language against his antagonists. But Brenz recalled the days when he and Osiander were working together for the expansion of the Evangelical faith in south Germany. He refused to take as seriously as most other Lutherans the differences between the new Koenigsberg theology and that of Wittenberg. Andreae signed memoranda composed by Brenz and the ecclesiastical staff of Duke Christoph which expressed this opinion in 1551 and 1553. From later utterances on the subject of Osiandrism it appears that Andreae may not have read and understood Osiander in the 1550s. After a period in which he tried to defend Osiander by interpreting his statements in a way that placed them much closer to Melanchthon's positions than Osiander intended, Andreae apparently decided that he must sharply condemn Osiander's doctrines to establish his documents of concord as the basis of Lutheran unity. This is true already in his "Confession" of 1568 and also in his *Six Christian Sermons.*

Controversies over the Lord's Supper and the Person of Christ

The conflict within Lutheranism which affected Andreae most in the years immediately preceding his first extended effort for Lutheran unity was the Sacramentarian conflict. Luther's disputes with Carlstadt, Zwingli, and others had set the tone for the most obvious and painful disagreements within the Evangelical camp in the early years of the Reformation. Even within the Wittenberg circle certain tensions over the concept of the real presence of Christ's body and blood in the Lord's Supper had developed in the closing years of Luther's life.

The geographical proximity of the Wuerttemberg church to the Swiss imposed upon it the necessity of dealing with the dispute between Luther and the Swiss. Johann Brenz was the single most influential churchman in the organization of the Lutheran reform of Wuerttemberg, even though he resided outside the domains of Duke Ulrich in the free imperial city of Schwaebisch-Hall. Brenz opposed Zwinglianism's influence in Wuerttemberg, and his personal views of the Sacrament were reinforced by treaty commitments made by Duke Ulrich which obligated him to oppose the Sacramentarianism of Zwingli and his followers.[25]

The controversy over the Sacrament simmered throughout Luther's life. After his death one of his students, Joachim Westphal, superintendent of the church of Hamburg, opened a new front on the battle over the Real Presence. The work of John Calvin in Geneva and his teaching on the Lord's Supper had aroused little comment and notice among Lutherans until Westphal's critique of the spread of Sacramentarian doctrines in his *Farrago of the Confusing Opinions, Which Differ from Each Other, on the Lord's Supper, Collected from the Books of the Sacramentarians,* published in 1552.[26] During the next several years the dispute continued in print between Calvin and Westphal and involved others on both sides before their public debate ended in 1558.

Soon thereafter the debate over the Real Presence arose in another quarter of the empire and in a form somewhat different from the paper war between Westphal and Calvin. The practical matter of shaping the doctrine for the church of the Palatinate was at the heart of the dispute between Tilemann Hesshus and Reformed theologians brought into the University of Heidelberg by Elector Frederick III. Frederick succeeded his cousin Otto Heinrich in 1559. Otto Heinrich had been a leader among the Lutheran princes, but Frederick led a movement to bring the Palatinate church to a position close to that of Calvin's Geneva. Frederick asked Melanchthon for an opinion on the definition of the Real Presence in an effort to mediate a dispute between Hesshus and Wilhelm Klebitz, a Heidelberg deacon inclined toward Calvin's position on the Lord's Supper. Melanchthon's memorandum disagreed with Hesshus's insistence that 1 Cor. 10:16 teaches that the bread in the Sacrament is the true body of Jesus Christ. The memorandum criticizes Hesshus for rejecting ancient fathers who called the bread a "symbol" or "antitype" of the body and urges use of the definition of the bread of the Sacrament as a "participation in the body of Christ" without interpretations which would imply that the bread becomes or is the body of Christ.[27] From his new pastorate in Magdeburg, Hesshus attacked this memorandum in two tracts the next year, but Melanchthon died and his disciples were reluctant to take public issue with Hesshus, their former friend and fellow student. Frederick III proceeded to establish Reformed doctrine in his land by bringing theologians of that persuasion to the theological faculty at Heidelberg and to important ecclesiastical posts in the Palatinate. With these theologians Andreae entered into debate over the doctrine of the Lord's Supper in 1564.

Andreae had worked hard in the late 1550s to create an accord which would end disputes over the Lord's Supper among the Evangelicals of Germany and Switzerland. The internal crisis over the sacramental views of a Wuerttemberg pastor, Bartholomaeus Hagen, had helped divert Andreae from this effort to find common ground with the Genevans in 1559. The Hagen matter was settled in a synod in Stuttgart in December 1559, which issued a *Confession and Report of the Theologians and Ministers in the Princedom of Wuerttemberg on the True Presence of the Body and Blood of Christ in the Holy Supper.*[28] The *Confession* established Brenz's concept of the ubiquity of Christ's human nature as a basic definition for the Wuerttemberg church. Brenz taught that the human nature of Christ shares the properties of His divine nature in the personal union and that therefore Christ's human body can be and is omnipresent everywhere.

Duke Christoph was not only interested in maintaining the doctrines of the Augsburg Confession as his theologians understood them; he was also interested in keeping the Evangelical princes of the empire united in that faith which had won legal status in 1555. Therefore he was concerned about the advance of Reformed deviations from that confession. Thus he took note of the publication of the Heidelberg Catechism in the Palatinate in 1563 and pressed for a colloquy between his own theologians and those of the Palatinate. At the Colloquy of Maulbronn, held in April 1564, Andreae played the leading role in defending the sacramental and Christological position laid down in the *Confession* of 1559. Not only did the dialog fail to produce accord between Heidelberg and Tuebingen; it also opened up a breach between Tuebingen and Wittenberg.

Duke Christoph had already expressed some doubts about the Wittenberg faculty. He nonetheless sent a copy of the minutes of the Maulbronn Colloquy, along with a copy of an academic disputation of Andreae's on the majesty of the man Christ, to the theologians at Wittenberg for an opinon. They replied with their *Censure of the*

Theologians on the Disputation of Johann Brenz and Jakob Andreae on the Majesty of Christ. They stated that they wished to abide by "orthodox" (patristic) Christology and asserted that the Wuerttembergers were introducing innovations in their concept of ubiquity. They wanted to keep Christology out of sacramental theology, and thus they tried to avoid the issues and framework of debate raised at the Maulbronn Colloquy. Though these differences did not develop into open antagonism at this point, this epistolary exchange in 1564 undoubtedly made it easier for Andreae to break with the Wittenbergers, with whom he had tried to create a common front, when their mutual antagonism once again emerged in 1570. However, that antagonism does not seem to have been in evidence at the end of the 1560s, when Andreae began his campaign for Lutheran unity.

Efforts Toward Dialog and Concord

Andreae was, of course, not the first who had sought to end the feuding among Evangelical theologians. Ever since the serious disputes over the Interims had begun to divide Lutheranism in Germany into openly antagonistic camps, Lutherans had tried to initiate the process of reconciliation.

Two patterns or approaches in the search for unity developed during the 1550s. The first depended to a great extent on the initiative and power of the princes and was supported by the Philippist party. The princes sought accord among their churches through meetings of the representatives of the Evangelical estates; often the princes themselves participated. At these meetings they usually tried to formulate a brief, concise, but seldom specific solution to the most pressing doctrinal issues under debate. The Philippists called for "amnesty" among Lutheran theologians so that old quarrels might be put away and forgotten.

The second approach to Lutheran unity was that of the Gnesio-Lutherans. Flacius and his comrades called for a conference of theologians, a synod or a colloquy, at which the various issues could be resolved. Such a synod would not grant amnesty for those in error; instead, it would condemn errors and those who propagated them, and it would call for those in error to repent publicly.

Pressure for Lutheran unity came not only from those who desired unity and harmony within the church. It also came indirectly from the Roman Catholics, eager to reverse the legal gains made by the

Evangelicals in 1555. The Evangelical princes felt it necessary to form a united front to combat that kind of pressure and to advance or at least secure the status of the faith of the Augsburg Confession in the empire. Some Evangelical German rulers, sympathetic toward the struggling Reformed church of France and the persecuted Protestants in the Netherlands, were anxious to form an Evangelical League of German princes to support those who opposed Rome in neighboring lands.

The second and third generation of Reformation princes had come to power in the wake of the Smalcaldic War. Duke Christoph of Wuerttemberg was among the most energetic in the search for a common stand among the Lutheran princes. In early 1556 he set in motion diplomatic maneuvers designed to reduce Gnesio-Lutheran opposition to a common Evangelical stand. His delegation arrived in Weimar in January to begin work on a settlement with the Gnesio-Lutheran advisers of Duke John Frederick the Middler. These advisers insisted on the condemnation of errors, and the effort was stymied.

Late in 1556 Flacius floated some "Gentle Proposals" for the settlement of differences between his party and the Wittenbergers, but the latter did not reply.[29] They did not view his proposals as very gentle, and they were still too suspicious of Flacius, the foreigner, the layman, who had had the audacity to mount such a strong attack against Melanchthon and those gathered around him.

At the end of 1556 a group of Lower Saxon Gnesio-Lutherans who were not closely associated with Flacius attempted to mediate the dispute between the Flacians in Magdeburg and the Philippists in Wittenberg. Flacius and his party assembled in January 1557 in the town of Coswig, and the Lower Saxons traveled back and forth to Wittenberg with messages from both sides. When their efforts could not bring the two sides together, Duke Johann Albrecht of Mecklenburg intervened, and through theologians from his staff the duke attempted to pull Flacius and Melanchthon together. Melanchthon agreed that most of Flacius' points were well taken, but he refused to cut his own throat in public. The colloquy by intermediary collapsed.[30]

The two factions of Saxon Lutheranism were caught up in the wider course of events. Emperor Ferdinand was pressing for a colloquy between adherents of Rome and adherents of the Augsburg Confession, and he arranged for the two confessions to meet for dialog in Worms in late 1557. The Evangelicals were confronted with a dilemma in their preparation for this colloquy. They were not united among themselves. The princes met in Frankfurt in June 1557 and tried to resolve the split in their ranks by suppressing it. That did not work.

An Evangelical delegation made up of Philippists and Gnesio-Lutherans, as well as representatives from Wuerttemberg, did sit down at the negotiating table in Worms with Roman Catholic theologians in August 1557. Melanchthon, Brenz, and others could not find common ground with the Gnesio-Lutheran delegation from ducal Saxony and two other Lower Saxon representatives. The latter insisted on the condemnation of sects which had arisen in recent years as a condition for the formation of a single Evangelical bloc which could talk as a unit with Roman Catholics. For a month wrangling continued, and finally the Gnesio-Lutherans withdrew. The Roman Catholics had agreed to the colloquy only under imperial pressure. They exploited the division among the Evangelicals, insisting that the colloquy could go on only between two parties, not between themselves and two separate Evangelical groups. They were glad when the colloquy collapsed before the end of the year.

The next year the Evangelical princes attempted to hammer out a basis for reconciliation at another meeting in the city of Frankfurt am Main. Melanchthon drew up articles on justification, good works, adiaphora, and the Lord's Supper. The three Evangelical electors as well as some other Evangelical princes subscribed the document. From the Gnesio-Lutherans the "Frankfurt Recess" brought forth only fierce denunciation for the failure of its brief statements to grasp the central issues of the debates over the topics it treated. They also objected to its failure to denounce some errors and some teachers of error.

Duke John Frederick the Middler of Saxony responded with a call for a synod of theologians at Magdeburg, but the other Evangelical princes brought political pressure to bear on the city council, and the plan collapsed. Instead, John Frederick had his theologians draw up the Book of Confutation (1559) to define and refute perversions of doctrine, sects, and errors. Flacius and his colleagues wanted to use the Book as a basis for further talks on unity with other Lutherans. But the Book did no more than arouse the other side and bring the wrath of Philip of Hesse down upon the ducal Saxon theologians. About this same time the Gnesio-Lutherans presented a Supplication to the Evangelical princes and estates.[31] This petition called for a synod which would define and refute error and

41

thus establish genuine Evangelical unity. The 51 theologians who signed the *Supplication* came mostly from central and northern Germany, and many had not been closely associated with the Flacian party. However, the *Supplication* was Gnesio-Lutheran in tone and in approach. The princes did not respond positively to its suggestion.

Instead, a number of princes gathered at Naumburg in early 1561. They resolved to subscribe to the Augsburg Confession as had the Evangelical princes 30 years earlier at Augsburg. They wanted to use the Augustana as the defining statement of their faith and wanted to address other pressing issues through a new preface, which they had drawn up. The preface was so vague and indeterminate that it provoked John Frederick the Middler and Duke Ulrich of Mecklenburg to walk out of the conference. This princely settlement brought no settlement at all.

Conferences of princes or their representatives took place throughout the next decade, but all were equally frustated in trying to make headway against the factors that separated the Saxon Lutherans. For the Saxons themselves were finding ever more to battle about. Controversy and suspicion create and fuel controversy and suspicion, and the 1560s witnessed no letup in the disputing between the Gnesio-Lutherans of Jena and the Philippists of Leipzig and Wittenberg. In October 1568 representatives from the two sides met in colloquy in Altenburg. Periodic meetings took place until the next March, when their differences over justification, free will, and good works again appeared insolvable. The Jena faculty published its own version of the meetings in 1570. They condemned the Philippists vehemently, and the Philippists answered in kind.[32] Thus the chief result of the colloquy was an increase of the divisive bitterness that had caused the colloquy.

By this time Jakob Andreae had already begun his drive toward concord, and a continuation of his life carries the story of Lutheran discord and the search for concord further.

Andreae and the Beginnings
of the Movement Toward Concord
Andreae's "Confession" and the Synod at Zerbst

The opportunity for mounting his personal campaign for harmony came in 1568 when Andreae was sent by Duke Christoph to Braunschweig-Wolfenbuettel to assist in the reorganization of its ecclesiastical life. Duke Heinrich, longtime papal supporter and fierce foe of Luther's Reformation, died in that year and was succeeded by his son Julius, a cousin of Duke Christoph. He asked Christoph to send him assistance for the task of restructuring the church of his lands according to an Evangelical model, and Andreae was dispatched to work with Martin Chemnitz, Evangelical preacher in the city of Braunschweig, to visit and reorganize the churches of Duke Julius' lands. At Christoph's urging Andreae took the opportunity to solicit Julius' aid in pressing for Lutheran unity, and Julius agreed to support Andreae in his bid to create a settlement through a brief confession which treated the five central issues about which the Lutherans had been disputing for 20 years. Andreae had probably brought with him from Wuerttemberg his "Confession and Brief Explanation of Certain Disputed Articles, Through Which Christian Unity May be Reached in the Churches Subscribing to the Augsburg Confession, and Scandalous, Wearisome Division May Be Set Aside." Duke Christoph died Dec. 28, 1568, but Julius and Christoph's son-in-law Landgrave William of Hesse promoted Andreae's tour of Evangelical Germany, which took place in 1569, as he tried to collect subscriptions to his "Confession." [33]

In the summer and autumn of 1569 Andreae took his "Confession" to Wittenberg and to the court of Elector August of Saxony as well as the courts of Elector Joachim of Brandenburg and his brother Margrave Hans of Kuestrin, of the dukes of Pomerania, Mecklenburg, Braunschweig-Lueneburg, Lauenberg, Holstein, and of the princes of Anhalt. He also visited the dowager queen of Denmark. He ventured into the citadel of recalcitrant Gnesio-Lutheranism, Weimar in ducal Saxony; and he sought support in cities such as Magdeburg, Hamburg, Luebeck, Lueneburg, and Bremen. [34]

43

He met with frustration, suspicion, and opposition as well as some encouragement on his journey. Georg Major seemed inclined to offer support in Wittenberg when Andreae visited there in early 1569. However, when Major's colleagues on the theological faculty met to study Andreae's "Confession" together (after the Altenburg Colloquy collapsed), they refused to endorse it. The general synod in Landgrave William's own lands did not support the "Confession" when it met in June 1569 but took a wait-and-see attitude toward Andreae's effort.[35]

Much of the outright opposition to Andreae's efforts came from the Gnesio-Lutherans. They charged that the fifth article of the "Confession" could easily be given a Zwinglian interpretation. So Andreae added a long appendix in which he condemned a figurative interpretation of the Words of Institution and taught the ubiquity of the human nature of Christ.[36] Andreae complained of the attacks of the "Spangenbergers," the ministerium of Mansfeld, so named for its superintendent Cyriakus Spangenberg, a lifelong supporter of Flacius.[37] He protested against the slander and abuse in a newly published work produced by the theologians at the ducal Saxon university at Jena—Hesshus, Wigand, Kirchener, and Coelestinus.[38] In early February 1570 he conferred with Duke John William of ducal Saxony, the protector of these antagonists, in Weimar. During his stay there the court preacher, Christoph Irenaeus, attacked him from the pulpit, as did Hesshus. Andreae interpreted Hesshus's remarks as an attack against Landgrave William and Duke Julius, and a small political imbroglio resulted.[39] In a letter to Landgrave William, Andreae observed that the theologians at Weimar had not only lost the Holy Spirit but their reason and common sense as well.[40] Andreae hoped to end such slander and quarreling through an assembly of theologians which he had persuaded William, Julius, and Elector August of Saxony to call.

In early April 1570 William and Julius invited a number of princes and cities to send representatives to a meeting at Zerbst in electoral Saxony to further Evangelical unity. Representatives from electoral Saxony, Brandenburg-Kuestrin, Hesse, Holstein, Anhalt, Hamburg, Lueneburg, and Luebeck joined Andreae, who represented Wuerttemberg unofficially and Braunschweig-Wolfenbuettel officially, at Zerbst for a two-day meeting in early May. The assembled theologians argued over proposals regarding confessional standards for Lutherans. The electoral Saxon representatives insisted that they would subscribe to no new confessional document, for none was needed. Andreae maintained a new document like his "Confession" was necessary since both sides in the intra-Lutheran controversies cited the Augustana against each other. The group argued over which documents should be regarded as definitive for Lutheranism, and they finally agreed that the Scriptures are interpreted by the ecumenical creeds, the Augsburg Confession, the Apology of the Augsburg Confession, the Smalcald Articles, Luther's catechisms, and other writings of Luther. The Wittenbergers thought that Melanchthon's writings, at least the *Corpus doctrinae Misnicum,*[41] ought to be regarded as confessional, but Andreae knew that that could only arouse the Gnesio-Lutherans to new heights of rage. So in the "Recess" which he composed as a summary agreement for the conference, he suggested that Melanchthon's works, along with those of Brenz, be recognized as helpful interpretations of the other confessional documents. The solution displeased the electoral Saxon delegation because it reduced Melanchthon's corpus to secondary status and put Brenz, the "Ubiquitist," on the same level as the Preceptor. As was their habit, however, they did not make this an issue and were content to let well enough alone. The conference ended in some confusion since the electoral Saxons were granted the right by the entire assembly to prepare their own "Recess" and then had this right rescinded after they had left the general assembly. Disagreement also arose over the significance of Andreae's official "Recess of Zerbst"; the electoral Saxon theologians could not regard it as a confession but only as an affirmation of their previous confessional integrity.[42]

As the synod at Zerbst closed, it seemed that Andreae and the Wittenbergers had been able to overcome their earlier antagonism over Christology. It appears that Andreae may really have believed that accord with the Wittenbergers had been reached; he seems not to have realized that the seeds of discord had been sown at the conference which he had hoped would proclaim and hasten the end of all discord among the Lutherans. He found out rather quickly. From Zerbst he proceeded to Wittenberg and there attended a disputation over theses which had just been published for a doctoral promotion at Leipzig.[43] In one thesis in particular the Saxons attacked the "Swabian" [44] Christology, and Andreae protested against their "unchristian, Mohammedan" beliefs. The Saxons insisted that they were only opposing Monophysitism in accord with Luther and the Augustana. Andreae began to realize that accord with the new Wittenberg theology could not be achieved without sacrificing what he understood to be Luther's and Brenz's doctrine of the Lord's Supper. This he refused to do.[45]

Other irritations and differences of viewpoint widened the rift Andreae was beginning to feel between himself and the Wittenbergers. The secrecy which followed Zerbst, the failure to publish its "Recess," naturally aroused suspicion among those who had not been invited to the meeting. The participating theologians and their princes were divided on the issue of publication. The Wittenbergers claimed the assembled theologians had agreed to keep silent concerning the outcome of the conference, and Elector August grumbled to William of Hesse that Andreae ought to be muzzled.[46] On the other hand, Andreae had wanted a public confession to affirm and proclaim unity, and Duke Julius supported him in this desire.[47] So in mid-summer 1570 Andreae issued his version of the proceedings at Zerbst in print. He thus unknowingly provoked the final break between himself and the theologians of electoral Saxony.[48]

The body of the *Report* which Andreae issued began with his recounting of difficulties which stood in the way of unity. He also defended his own calling to the task of establishing unity with references to the support of Dukes Christoph and Julius and Landgrave William, and then his *Report* traces the journey which took him to various cities and lands in pursuit of unity in 1569. This section recites both his successes and his frustrations and failures. Andreae reacted quite sharply to the opposition of the Gnesio-Lutherans in Weimar, particularly that of Hesshus, recounting the latter's criticism of his mission in detail. Andreae also defended the Wittenberg delegation to the Altenburg Colloquy and criticized the Gnesio-Lutherans for their lack of desire for Christian peace and unity, as it had been displayed at that colloquy.[49]

A list of 54 nasty names by which Andreae had been labeled by his detractors is printed as the preface to another section that offers a strong defense of his mission and of his own motives in undertaking it. The publication of this list illustrates not only Andreae's difficulties but also the frustration and disappointments he was experiencing. He tied the defense of this mission closely to the support it was receiving from the princes. By doing this he was reinforcing the impression that the Gnesio-Lutherans stood in opposition to the Evangelical rulers. He also answered specific charges against himself in regard to Osiandrism, Majorism, Zwinglianism, and other errors.[50]

46

Following this apologia for his mission Andreae set forth the events of May 1570 at Zerbst. There, he reported, the assembled theologians had invented nothing new but had simply renewed their former consensus on the teaching of Scripture, the creeds, the Augsburg Confession and its Apology, the Smalcald Articles, and the catechisms of Luther. He then followed this account with a discussion of the disputation held at Wittenberg in May 1570 concerning the person and natures of Christ. The *Report* notes the offense which the views of the Wittenbergers caused to the visiting theologians because the Wittenbergers seemed to be denying that the human nature of Christ shares the attributes of the divine nature. The visitors and the Wittenberg faculty discussed the matter at length, and Andreae printed in the *Report* the view upon which he thought they had agreed.[51] Apparently that view was one with which he was very comfortable but one which the Wittenbergers could not honestly permit to be attributed to themselves. So they began to take private exception as they expressed their anger at the publication of the *Report*. The *Report* closed with another statement of Andreae's basic confession and his further suggestions for establishing Lutheran concord.

Andreae must have seen coming the imminent collapse of his drive for concord, which had begun with his "Confession" and which he had thought would climax near triumph at Zerbst. As he was returning from Braunschweig to Wuerttemberg in September 1570, he stopped in Kassel, where Landgrave William informed him of Elector August's displeasure with his publication of the "Recess of Zerbst." Two letters to the landgrave from the following February and March reveal Andreae's growing bitterness against the Wittenbergers; it stands in marked contrast to the hope with which he had viewed that faculty just a year earlier. He complained to the prince about the poor thanks he had gotten from the Wittenbergers for all he had done for them; he had reaped only suspicion and mockery for his troubles.[52] The second letter conveys the Wittenbergers' critique of Andreae's *Report* on Zerbst with Andreae's own comments on that critique in the margin. He denied that he had misrepresented the actions of the synod when he prepared his *Report* for print. He accused the Wittenbergers of running off with the papists at the time of the Interims (a charge the Gnesio-Lutherans had made for over 20 years). An entire change in his outlook and his understanding of the Evangelical scene comes in another marginal comment. The Wittenbergers had stated in their critique that the articles of Andreae's *Report* were "incomplete, murky, doubtful, and in some places more of a

47

Flacian[53] opinion." Andreae observed alongside the last phrase: "That's where the whole matter lies and is to be found. They [the Flacianists] are too Lutheran and not papistic or Calvinistic enough for you."[54] That phrase is a signpost pointing in a new direction for Andreae. Setting out in that new direction, he composed his *Six Sermons*.

Andreae's Six Christian Sermons

After the failure of Zerbst, in late 1570, Andreae returned home to Wuerttemberg and assumed once more his duties at the court and university of young Duke Ludwig. In 1572 one of Julius' theologians, Nikolaus Selnecker, dedicated his *Institution of the Christian Religion* to Ludwig, and in its preface he rejoiced at the unity of faith and teaching which Wuerttemberg and Braunschweig shared. He also praised Andreae's contributions to the Evangelical Church of Braunschweig.[55] Andreae responded by writing the *Six Sermons*. In some ways they resemble 33 sermons he had actually preached in Esslingen in 1567, when the Tuebingen faculty held classes in that city during an outbreak of the plague in Tuebingen. In these *Thirty-three Sermons on the Most Important Divisions in the Christian Religion, Which Exist Between Papists, Lutherans, Zwinglians, Schwenckfelders, and Anabaptists,*[56] Andreae outlined for his hearers the differences between the teachings of Scripture and what he viewed as its misinterpretation by those groups. The *Six Sermons* dealt with the five Lutheran disputes he had treated in his "Confession" and with five additional disputes in much the same way that he had treated questions at issue between Lutherans and those outside Lutheranism in the *Thirty-three Sermons.*

It might be said that the *Six Sermons* are directly descended from Andreae's "Confession" of 1568; he had undoubtedly introduced approaches, examples, and phrases into the discussion of the "Confession" which he used in the *Six Sermons.*[57] However, the 99 pages of the *Six Sermons* contain about 75 times as many words as the "Confession." They employ two new methods: specific condemnation of false teachers by name, and use of the catechism as an aid for deciding the disputes under discussion. These new methods and the greatly expanded discussions of the divisions among the Lutherans indicate that the *Six Sermons* represent a new, fresh start on Andreae's part in the direction of concord.

In the preface, dated Feb. 17, 1573, Andreae dedicated his *Six Sermons* to his patron, Duke Julius, who had invested so much in his earlier travels in pursuit of concord. The preface explains Andreae's mission and the situation in which he was trying to carry it out.

Andreae felt compelled to defend his own calling to his task and the task itself in this preface. Particularly the staff of Duke John William of Saxony had been quick and severe in their judgments against Andreae while he was seeking subscriptions to his "Confession." He answered their accusations by insisting that he had never approved any falsification of doctrine in words or in essential content and had never covered up or spread such falsification.[58] Since Zerbst the Wittenbergers had also been attacking Andreae, and he reacted to their charges that he was not furthering the common cause but just pursuing the matter for his own sake, for personal glory.[59] Andreae began his defense by citing 1 Cor. 9:19: "Although I am free from all men, I have made myself a slave to all, that I might win the more." Under that motif, following Paul's example, Andreae was setting out on "the necessary task of once again restoring wherever possible Christian unity among the theologians of the Augsburg Confession without any compromise of the divine truth." He had not set out to work for unity without a proper divine call, he insisted, or just for his own sake. He was performing this service "only out of dutiful obedience to the Christian and godly princes by whom I was sent for the benefit and welfare of the whole church of God."[60] Andreae believed that princes had a God-given duty to govern the affairs of the church and to root out troublemakers within it.[61] He also cited his acquaintance with all the churches of the Augsburg Confession, formed on his visits to them over the past years, as part of his peculiar suitability for the task. Furthermore, Andreae assured Duke Julius, all who correctly understood what he was doing had not only approved the project but had also expressed gratitude for the princely support Julius had given to Andreae's efforts. They had all urged Andreae to push forward without regard for the gossip, insults, and ridicule he had had to suffer. Thus Andreae was attempting once more to establish concord through the *Six Sermons.*[62]

Andreae also felt compelled to defend his efforts in behalf of unity against those who said that unity in the church would never be achieved anyway. Here he was again referring to the ducal Saxon party.[63] Their view ran counter to a concern that had dominated Andreae's thinking throughout much of his career. He had actively sought Christian unity even while attacking errors within Christendom. Charges and insinuations from non-Lutherans that the Lutherans were hopelessly split among themselves had provoked him to write a *Report on the Unity and Disunity of the Theologians of the Christian Augsburg Confession* after the diet at Augsburg in 1559.[64] Again in 1573 Andreae was reacting against the accusation of the papal party that there were not 10 who subscribed to the Augsburg Confession who actually agreed on its teaching. Andreae insisted that except for a few theologians who had created the 10 controversies he discussed, the several thousand churchmen of the Augustana were united in one faith. Andreae was concerned that the slanders of these adversaries be met with a declaration of unity, which would bring the Lutherans comfort and joy. Around such a declared standard of unity true Lutherans could gather, and the deceivers within the Lutheran camp would have to stop their braying and would be revealed. Then, Andreae believed, the sweet and pleasant unity which the Evangelical churches knew at the time of the presentation of the Augsburg Confession in 1530 would return.[65] (By 1573 the Evangelicals were already looking back to a golden age.) The purpose of the restoration of unity, according to Andreae, was not just to affirm God's will that the church be one, but also to confound the adversaries of the truth outside and also inside the Lutheran camp.

The Lord Himself had inspired this effort, Andreae reminded Duke Julius, implying that the failure of his first attempt at restoring Lutheran unity need not mean that his second attempt would fail. Just as Christ told His mother at Cana: "My hour has not yet come," so He had spoken to the German Evangelicals, who must now wait for God's good time (Eccl. 3:1) to restore the unity they sought. They could only plant and water; God would have to give the increase (1 Cor. 3:6).[66]

That process of planting and watering the tender shoot of Evangelical unity involved facing squarely the obstacles to that unity. Within the sermons themselves Andreae did not suggest that all these disputes had been caused by one of the two parties that were opposing his efforts, but rather dwelt on the specific individuals or groups involved in the specific disputes. In the preface, however, he pointed to two parties who in 1573 were frustrating the drive for concord among Lutherans.

The first party, Andreae conceded, did want to suppress divisive errors, but its members also wanted to suppress faithful servants in the churches of the Augsburg Confession. He identified this group in the margin of the preface as the theologians of Thuringia (ducal Saxony), Mansfeld, and Regensburg.[67] But his slap on the wrist of this group was quite mildly stated, and in the *Six Sermons* he made one major methodological accommodation to the Gnesio-Lutherans of ducal Saxony and in general supported their doctrinal position.

The methodological concession involved the matter of condemnations. Both the Philippist-princely party and the Flacianists had agreed in the 1550s and 1560s that false doctrine must be condemned. But Flacius and his comrades had always insisted that false teachers, not just false doctrines, be specifically condemned.[68] Andreae's "Confession" had included the rejection of "those who teach otherwise," but it had mentioned no one by name. In the text of the *Six Sermons* Andreae also disregarded names and labeled the sides in each controversy as "the one party" and "the other party" as a general rule. (The exception came in the sixth sermon, where he spoke directly of the "new theologians in Wittenberg."[69]) However, even though personal condemnations were not placed in the text itself, the names of theologians who supported the accepted and the rejected positions were printed in the margin alongside their views. Andreae thus could say, on the one hand, that he was not using personal condemnation in the declaration upon which he hoped to base unity. But on the other hand he could point out, since the printed version of the sermons is the primary version, that he was clearly demonstrating whose interpretation on each given question was to be accepted and whose was to be rejected.

In the sermon on the righteousness of faith in God's sight, Osiander's name is associated with the one party while the correct view is assigned to "the theologians of the Augsburg Confession, Dr. Moerlin, and others."[70] Joachim Moerlin had been one of the East Prussian theologians who had opposed Osiander early in that controversy. He had also been closely associated with the Gnesio-Lutherans of Lower Saxony. Georg Major's proposition "Good works are necessary for salvation" and Nikolaus von Amsdorf's proposition "Good works are harmful to salvation" were both condemned, and names were named in the margin of the text. Andreae saw as much danger in the so-called Epicurean faith, which does not devote itself to good works at all, as he did in the hypocritical reliance on good works.[71] Besides, Amsdorf, the revered "uncle" of the Gnesio-Lutherans, had alienated himself from Hesshus and Wigand, the ducal Saxon theological leaders whom Andreae was trying to court in early 1573. Andreae also rejected the opinion of Flacius in his discussion of original sin.[72] He held instead to the opposing position expressed by Hesshus and Wigand, even though they so vehemently opposed his drive for concord.[73] In commenting on the freedom of the will, Andreae included Flacius with Hesshus, Wigand, and the Gnesio-Lutherans Nikolaus Gallus and Simon Musaeus as those whose judgment ought to be respected, against that of the Philippist Viktorin Strigel and his synergistic followers.[74]

Flacius, Gallus, Hesshus, Wigand, and the Lower Saxons were again mentioned as those who upheld the correct position in the Adiaphoristic controversy against "one part of the Wittenbergers and the papist theologians."[75] The same group of Gnesio-Lutherans presented the proper judgment, according to Andreae's marginal comment, in the dispute over the definition of the Gospel and the place of repentance in that definition. The rejected opinion was that held by "Dr. Pezel and the Wittenberg theologians."[76]

The marginal comments reinforce the statements of the text in Andreae's sixth sermon, on the Lord's Supper and the person of Christ. In the historical introduction section of that sermon Andreae charged that the Wittenbergers had come out from behind the bushes at long last to support the Zwinglian view of Christ's person, and he observed in the margin: "The new theologians at Wittenberg have given public support to the Zwinglians."[77]

This aggressively anti-Wittenberg stance in the sixth sermon was heralded already in the preface. Andreae only briefly mentioned the party which blocked unity by condemning the faithful servants of the church, the Gnesio-Lutherans. He dwelt at some length on the other group. His description bristles with the anger born of betrayal. For at Zerbst Andreae had believed that the Wittenbergers had been won for his camp; he had set himself up for attack from the Gnesio-Lutherans through his defense of the theologians of electoral Saxony. They, he now recalled, had told him in front of witnesses at Zerbst that they were totally satisfied with the Swabian and Lower Saxon churches, particularly with Andreae's friend Johann Brenz. Later they were found condemning Andreae's activities in behalf of concord and rejecting the doctrine of Brenz and Luther on the Lord's Supper and the person of Christ.[78] Their rejection of Brenz's Christology was only the latest of a number of roadblocks they had thrown in the path toward Lutheran concord. They were also forbidding the sale of books composed by servants of the churches of the Augsburg Confession, thus bewitching and poisoning the youth at their own schools. Only one thing could be done to counter them. The authorities in electoral Saxony would not act until they understood what was really going on. To hasten that realization Andreae urged that the churches and schools which taught pure doctrine should declare their unity.[79] He conceived of his effort toward concord also as an instrument which would drive those in error out of electoral Saxony by enlightening their victim. Whatever factors were actually involved, Elector August of Saxony did drive Andreae's antagonists out of their offices the next year—with a vengeance.[80]

Andreae's shift toward the Gnesio-Lutherans can be seen not only in his adopting the method of personal condemnation but also in the way he viewed the nature of the Lutheran controversies as well. In 1570 he expressed his opinion that the controversies were largely—though certainly not completely—battles over words, caused by the arrogance, ambition, pride, and envy of the theologians.[81] In the *Six Sermons* he recognized, too, that some of the disputes among Lutherans had been largely battles over words, e.g., the Majoristic controversy. But the phrases "Good works are necessary for salvation" and "Good works are harmful to salvation" were to be rejected even though both sides knew that only faith in Christ justifies and saves, and that this faith is not dead but living through love. For St. Paul commanded Timothy to hold onto the pattern of sound words (2 Tim. 1:13); that means that Christians should not only teach edifying doctrine but also use salutary words and ways of speaking, which do not give rise to quarreling, controversy, or error, Andreae insisted.[82] Furthermore, with his discovery that the Wittenbergers had rejected the Christology that he held, Andreae found another very serious doctrinal division within the Lutheran camp. He could see shades not only of Nestorianism but also of Arianism in the position of the Wittenbergers.[83] He had never said that all the disputes among the Lutherans were merely battles over words, but now he was beginning to share the Gnesio-Lutherans' view of just how serious the error involved in some of these controversies was.

Andreae's *Six Sermons* mark a definite shift in the way he viewed his situation and in the way he sought concord. No longer did he try to hold inoffensive middle ground between the Flacianists and the Philippists. He joined with the Gnesio-Lutherans in 1573 in forthright condemnation of the Wittenbergers, and in so doing he temporarily adopted an important part of the Gnesio-Lutheran method of seeking concord in the church. He also came to share their understanding of the nature and seriousness of the controversies within the Lutheran churches.

Andreae did not trim his beliefs to woo the Gnesio-Lutheran party, although their positions may well have influenced the way he formulated and dealt with certain questions.[84] Andreae found himself drawn toward the Gnesio-Lutherans when he discovered a genuine conflict between his own beliefs and those of the Wittenbergers, as their position finally became clear to him. He reacted angrily against what he regarded as their betrayal of Luther and their rejection of Brenz on the doctrine of the person of Christ. He reacted with a fury against their betrayal of him in their transformation of seeming support into firm opposition to his plans for concord. He decided that that part of the Gnesio-Lutheran party which had separated itself from Flacius agreed with the Swabian church on the important issues under discussion among the theologians of the Augsburg Confession.

But the *Six Sermons* were not written for Gnesio-Lutheran theologians, however much they may have been directed toward those listening from Jena and Weimar. The *Sermons* were composed for the average Christian layman and his pastor, who had found the controversies among the theologians an offense to their faith. The form in which Andreae presented each issue reflects this concern. He reviewed briefly the history of the dipute and set down the basic arguments of each side, with the Scriptural support they claimed. Then, through the use of the catechism, he showed the layman how to decide which party was teaching correctly.

Andreae had always been concerned about the instruction of the simple Christian layman. His first publication, in 1557, was his *Short and Simple Statement Concerning the Lord's Supper, and How an Ordinary Christian Should Conduct Himself in the Long and Drawn-out Controversy Which Has Arisen over It.*[85] The next year he composed a *Simple Report, How Every Christian Should Give Answer out of His Catechism, Why He No Longer Attends Mass.*[86] His *Thirty-three Sermons* had dealt with differences between other Christian groups and the Evangelicals on a popular level.

In the *Thirty-three Sermons* Andreae discussed the plight of the layman facing the theological disputes of his day. Most Christians could not read or write and were unable to dispute with Satan or man, Andreae observed. Others read the Scriptures but did not have the gift of the Holy Spirit, which is necessary for interpretation. As a result the learned were leading the simple astray. The layman's weapon against such deception was his faith, which must always be coupled with God's Word for the Word to be properly understood. Christ should be the Christian's rock which he hurls with the sling of his faith against the devil's head. What is that faith? Andreae asked. It is the 12 articles of the creed; it is the simple catechism.[87]

This concern for the layman surfaced again in his drive for concord on the basis of the "Confession." He noted in his sermon on March 22, 1570, in Dresden that the controversies within Lutheranism had led laymen astray and harmed them. The layman who reads at best only an occasional German tract cannot gain an understanding from what he reads nor from the slanders he hears from the pulpit, Andreae said.[88]

So in the *Six Sermons* Andreae turned to the catechism,[89] particularly to the creed, as the instrument by which the layman might determine who was right in the controversy under discussion. He did not appeal to the catechism as the deposit of the wisdom of the church; his is in no way an argument from tradition. He appealed instead to something that might be called "Christian common sense"—simply the analogy of faith. In each sermon, after outlining the arguments of each side, with a battery of Scriptural proof passages used by each, Andreae presented a little dialog between layman and author. The layman asks: "I hear, to be sure, that both parties cite Holy Scripture. Who will tell me which party speaks correctly or incorrectly about this matter? For I am a simple layman and can neither read nor write. Whom should I believe and follow?" Andreae answers: "Here a simple layman should take the simple creed of the children and seek in it his righteousness"—from the first sermon, on Osiandrism. There he finds in the sentence "I believe in the forgiveness of sins" the assurance that God will not let him suffer for his sins but will forgive him by grace. The layman then looks at the whole of the Second Article and finds no mention of the indwelling righteousness of God, which Osiander equated with the righteousness of the sinner. Instead, from the Second Article the layman learns that his righteousness consists in the obedience, suffering, and death of Jesus Christ.[90]

In his use of the creed Andreae usually did not refer to anything but the words of the creed itself. Twice, however, in his third sermon he referred to Luther's explanations of the articles of the creed. In discussing whether original sin has become the substance of man, Andreae paraphrased and summarized Luther's explanation of the First Article, to demonstrate that God, who created all things, did not create original sin. Andreae quoted the explanation to the Third Article directly: "I cannot by my own reason or strength believe in Jesus Christ, my Lord, or come to Him . . ." in refuting the synergists.[91]

He also used other elements of the catechism. The First Commandment gives the layman direction when faced with the dilemma of suffering or permitting adiaphora to be imposed upon him in violation of Christian freedom and at the cost of a clear confession of the truth. Andreae searched the entire catechism through to ascertain whether anything but the Law accuses the sinner of his sin. Since only the Ten Commandments point to man's sin, and since Christians still sin, the layman must reject the antinomianism of John Agricola. In arriving at the definition of the Gospel as solely the proclamation of forgiveness of sins, Andreae consulted the Office of the Keys, and there he found his definition of the Gospel.[92]

This appeal to the catechism is not an appeal to an authority above or alongside Scripture. The catechism is merely the tool with which the layman, unskilled in the techniques of exegesis, may find his way through the maze constructed by conflicting interpretations of passages from the Bible and by uses of one passage by one side and another by the other to support opposing viewpoints. Andreae's layman asks at one point if the Holy Spirit speaks against Himself, and Andreae replies in such a way as to make it clear that he does not believe the creed is a final arbitrator over Scripture. It is just that not all who read and use Scripture have the gift of proper interpretation which the Holy Spirit alone provides.[93] The catechism enables even the simple layman to determine which side is reading Scripture correctly and which is misinterpreting it, according to Andreae.

On the Way to Lutheran Concord

The *Six Sermons* mark the turning point in the effort of Jakob Andreae and many other Lutherans to reestablish concord among those who subscribed to the Augsburg Confession in the last third of the 16th century. The *Six Sermons* convinced key Lutheran churchmen that Andreae was more than just a compromiser, that he was indeed a confessor. Westphal, Chemnitz, and Chytraeus read the *Six Sermons* and decided that on the basis of this document concord could be sought and reached. They combined their energy and effort with Andreae's and that of many others who longed for harmony, and a new drive toward concord began. The *Six Christian Sermons* were the basis from which Andreae constructed his "Swabian Concord," which incorporated suggestions from several other theologians, including Martin Chemnitz. He had asked Duke Julius to request a new form for the articles of faith upon which agreement was to be built, that of thesis and antithesis, as the Gnesio-Lutherans had insisted for some time. By the end of November 1573 Andreae had his new "Concord" ready. It won approval in Wuerttemberg. A year later the Lower Saxon theologians had reviewed the document and returned it to Andreae with changes in a new statement, the "Swabian-Saxon Concord." It, along with another formula composed by another committee from Wuerttemberg, the "Maulbronn Formula," laid the foundation for the "Torgic Book," which was amended into the "Bergic Book" during the course of 1576 and 1577. This "Bergic Book" became the Solid Declaration of the Formula of Concord.[94]

The prominence of the catechetical argument receded in the revisions and reworkings of 1573—77, and the personal condemnations disappeared, though catechism and condemnation of error survived the conferences which forged the Formula. The theological concerns and expressions of others altered and supplemented Andreae's views and phrases in the Formula's final version. However, in and through his *Six Christian Sermons* Andreae not only helped create the text of the Formula of Concord but also fostered the climate in which such a formula could be written and accepted. Without the help of princes his efforts could hardly have reached fruition, but without Jakob Andreae the princes had made little headway in forging Lutheran unity during nearly two decades of trying to stop theologians' disputes. Andreae was able to initiate the movement toward concord in part by emphasizing his pastoral concern for pastors and laypeople who were being offended by controversy and deceived by false teachers, and in part by taking his stance as a confessor of the central teachings of Scripture as he understood them from reading Luther and talking with Brenz. Both these factors—his pastoral concern and his confessional stance—put him in the mainstream of 16th-century Lutheranism. Both help account for the success of his second venture in pursuit of concord.

TRANSLATIONS

CONFESSION AND BRIEF EXPLANATION OF CERTAIN DISPUTED ARTICLES, THROUGH WHICH CHRISTIAN UNITY MAY BE REACHED IN THE CHURCHES SUBSCRIBING TO THE AUGSBURG CONFESSION, AND SCANDALOUS, WEARISOME DIVISION MAY BE SET ASIDE[1]

Article I
On Justification Through Faith

Concerning the article on the justification of the poor sinner in God's sight, we believe, teach, and confess on the basis of God's Word and the position of our Christian Augsburg Confession that the poor, sinful person is justified in God's sight—that is, he is pronounced free and absolved of his sins and receives forgiveness for them—only through faith, because of the innocent, complete, and unique obedience and the bitter sufferings and death of our Lord Jesus Christ, not because of the indwelling, essential righteousness of God or because of his own good works, which either precede or result from faith. We reject all doctrines contrary to this belief and confession. For although God, Father, Son, and Holy Spirit, who is essential righteousness Himself, dwells in believers and impels them to do right and to live according to His divine will, nevertheless God's indwelling does not make them perfect in this life. Therefore they cannot be considered righteous in God's sight because of this indwelling. Instead, all their consolation is to be found alone in the unique and innocent obedience and the bitter suffering and death of our Lord Jesus Christ. This obedience is credited to all repentant sinners as righteousness in God's sight.

Article II
On Good Works

Concerning good works we believe, teach, and confess on the basis of the divine Word and the position of the Christian Augsburg Confession that we do not become righteous nor are we saved through good works, as the term is commonly understood. For Christ has earned salvation as well as righteousness (that is, the forgiveness of sins) with His innocent obedience, suffering, and death alone. This is credited to all believers as righteousness only through faith. We reject all who teach otherwise. Along with this we steadfastly teach that whoever wants to be a true Christian and wants to be saved eternally is obligated to do good works and should do them—not to earn or obtain salvation through them, but to demonstrate his faith and gratitude for the merits of Christ and also to demonstrate the obedience he owes to God, as it is written: "If you live according to the flesh, you will die, but if you put to death the deeds of the flesh, you will live" (Rom. 8:13). We also reject all those who teach that righteousness in God's sight is credited to us on account of the works which we perform out of faith, and that salvation is earned and obtained through them.

Article III
On the Free Will

Concerning the free will of man after the fall, we believe, teach, and confess on the basis of God's Word and the position of the Christian Augsburg Confession that we poor sinners are not just mortally wounded through sin and transgression (insofar as rebirth, spiritual and heavenly matters, and works which please God the Lord are concerned); we also, as St. Paul shows, are completely dead in this regard. Thus we are not even capable of conceiving of something good. Instead, the Lord causes us both to will and to carry out that will through the Holy Spirit, so that the honor belongs to God alone. He, out of His pure grace, has made us alive and righteous and has saved us from death in sin. Nevertheless, since man is not a block of wood but is still a reasoning creature even after the fall, he has a free, though weak, will in externals. In divine and spiritual matters and in the mysteries of the Kingdom of God his understanding is totally blind, so that he does not perceive the things of God's Spirit. They are foolishness to him, and he cannot discern them when he is asked about spiritual matters. Thus his will is held captive and has died in regard to the good. If God does not create a new will in him, he cannot, out of himself and his own powers, restore himself, nor can he accept the grace of God shown us in Christ. We reject those who teach otherwise.

Article IV
On Indifferent Matters, Called Adiaphora

Concerning ceremonies and ecclesiastical usages, which God has neither commanded nor forbidden in His Word, we believe, teach, and confess on the basis of God's Word and the position of the Augsburg Confession that they should be made subservient to, not superior to, the pure doctrine of God's Word. If a denial of the Christian religion, doctrine, and confession is associated with or attached to the acceptance of such things, so that they are no longer free, they should be abandoned and may not be used with a good conscience. We reject all who teach otherwise.

Article V
On the Holy Supper

Concerning the holy sacrament of the body and blood of our Lord Jesus Christ, we believe, teach, and confess on the basis of God's Word and the position of the Christian Augsburg Confession that in it, with the bread and wine, the true body and blood of our Lord Jesus Christ, who is present in a heavenly way unfathomable by human reason, is distributed and received by all who use this sacrament according to His command and institution. We believe, teach, and confess also that not only true believers and genuine Christians but also the godless and unrepentant hypocrites, who are baptized and intermingled among saved Christians, receive the true body and blood of Christ in the holy sacrament—of course, to their judgment. That judgment is either temporal punishment for those who repent or eternal punishment for those who persist in their sinful life and do not turn to God. For Christ is not only a true savior but also a judge. He brings judgment upon the unrepentant, who are intermingled among true believers in the use of this sacrament, just as He also brings life to the true Christians. Thus, the presence of Christ in the sacrament does not depend on the worthiness or unworthiness of the individual who distributes or uses the sacrament but on Christ's word, which established and instituted it. We reject all who teach otherwise concerning this sacrament.

Six Christian Sermons

On the Divisions

Which Have Continued to Surface

Among the Theologians of the Augsburg Confession

From 1548 Until This Year 1573,

How a Simple Pastor and a Common Christian Layman

Should Deal with Them on the Basis of His Catechism,

So That They Do Not Become a Scandal

For Them

By

Jakob Andreae, Doctor, Provost at Tuebingen,

and the Chancellor

of the University of Tuebingen

You will find, Christian reader,

the content of each sermon

on the pages immediately following

Printed at Tuebingen

by Georg Gruppenbach

1573

To his serene highness, prince and lord, Julius, duke of Brunswick and Lueneburg, my gracious prince and lord, etc.

Serene Highness, Prince, gracious Lord. St. Paul writes to the Corinthians: "Although I am free from all men, I have made myself a slave to all, that I might win the more" (1 Cor. 9:19). With these words the holy apostle has set himself up as an example and model for all faithful servants of the church; according to his example they should exercise their office for the good of the church.

As an unworthy servant of the Word of God I recognize that I am bound to this example in my entire calling, particularly in pursuing the salutary, praiseworthy, and highly necessary task of once again restoring—through God's grace—wherever possible Christian unity among the theologians of the Augsburg Confession without any compromise of the divine truth. This task has been promoted at no small cost in a most Christian and princely manner by Your Princely Grace ever since the death of the serene and high-born prince and lord, Lord Christoph, duke of Wuerttemberg and Teck, count of Montbeliard, of praiseworthy and blessed memory.

Two obstacles intervened so that this task was not fully accomplished with everyone involved (at the synod of Zerbst) through the written declarations which—it was hoped—could be obtained on the basis of the oral declarations from all sides (at Zerbst) and the resulting Christian Recess of Zerbst. The one party was concerned to suppress through these proceedings all the divisive corruptions, errors, and falsifications of the doctrine of the holy Gospel which had been introduced into the churches of the Augsburg Confession by a very few theologians who subscribed to the confession; these errors had been shoved in under a cloak, covered up, and passed over in silence for 20 or more years. This party wanted to suppress some faithful servants and guardians of these churches as well.[2] The other party used such fine words and made such a declaration to me, in the presence of the secular counselors who were sent along with me, that I took real pleasure at their words. For they stated plainly that they were totally satisfied with the Swabian and Lower Saxon churches, particularly with Dr. Brenz,[3] as a person who brought great benefits to the church of God and as a faithful follower of Dr. Luther in every article of our religion. But later they expressed themselves much differently concerning my activities and that of many other godly Christians.[4] Because of this even many sincere men who had opposed this endeavor previously did not want to be associated with their sin and their publicly stated errors and therefore subscribed not just in writing but also in public print to the documents which were suggested as documents that set forth pure doctrine: first of all, the writings of the prophets and apostles, the only rule and guide of the truth; then the three creeds, Apostolic, Nicene, and Athanasian; the Augsburg Confession; the Apology; the Smalcald Articles; and Luther's catechisms. These documents were incorporated into the Recess of Zerbst as those which are read by the learned and the unlearned and which give direction and definition for the easy recognition and censure of all errors.

It is my intention to follow dutifully the example and model of the holy apostle in this great task which I have taken upon myself. I did so not for my own sake without a proper divine call; I have performed the task with my insignificant service only out of dutiful obedience to the Christian and godly princes by whom I was sent for the benefit and welfare of the whole church of God. From both groups I put up with no little insulting, mockery, and ridicule, which I have borne until now with patience, by God's grace.

To carry out this intention I have ignored all previous ingratitude and have not stopped trying gladly and willingly to make myself the servant of everyone, even of this latter group, to further this salutary and highly necessary task and to erase the suspicion of the first group (who are otherwise one with us on all articles of our Christian religion). I wanted to defend this work not just with fine phrases but with a detailed explanation of all the strife which has come upon the churches of the Augsburg Confession, as was necessary. I have composed such an explanation in a few simple sermons for simple pastors and laymen, in the same manner in which I preached at Esslingen against the papists, Zwinglians, Schwenckfelders, and Anabaptists.[5] From this it is obvious that my intention has never been, nor is now, to justify, spare, cover up, or cloak the tiniest corruption or falsification of pure doctrine in one or more articles of faith through a superficial harmonization, as widespread rumor has it. That I can prove, with God as my witness, to Your Princely Grace and many other Christians without hiding anything. Since I sought this declaration of unity among the teachers of the Augsburg Confession through this task which was set before me in a proper manner and only for the purpose of promoting divine truth, I hope they will be satisfied with this. I hope since they love Christian unity no less than divine truth, they will not delay this endeavor any longer nor let the clear declaration of Christian concord on the basic foundation of Christian doctrine slip further away.

Now to the second party. For many years this party has unfortunately caused scandalous dissension. Recently it has been pleading, urging, and admonishing in a friendly fashion on many sides in regard to just everything. But with its unfounded account of this matter it has not only hindered this Christian endeavor; on top of these previous obstacles this party also introduced a new controversy on the person of Christ (which had long lain inside them, but before now they did not dare make it public).[6] Through this they paved the way into the churches of the Augsburg Confession not just for Zwinglianism but also for other

63

heresies. They have the impudence to set aside Luther's blessed foundation which he set down against this error and heresy. They forbid the sale of whatever the pure churches and schools and their servants compose and print against the new basis of doctrine which they are dreaming up. Thus their poor young people, cultivated in such poison, are not aware of their deception and are not being forewarned. Therefore they are not kept at a distance from it. Finally they become captivated by this error and are completely poisoned. They must be commended to the Almighty until the time He chooses, when the authorities in that place at length receive reports of the basic facts in the matter and conduct a proper investigation. Without doubt they will know what to do then.[7] That would undoubtedly take place all the sooner if the pure churches and schools would declare clearly, sincerely, and openly their Christian and godly unity in relation to each other (as, praise God, this unity is maintained no less in Lower Saxony than throughout all Swabia) in a public document, not just on bits and pieces but on the whole of Christian doctrine. All pious Christians would declare this unity with their own signatures and thus create comfort and joy in the face of the many sorts of slanders we receive from our adversaries. This would expose the basic position of such deceivers, who in this current state of dissension suppress and easily conceal their braying and writing in our church. Then, as is fitting, the school they really belong to would be identified, and accordingly it would be made clear to one and all in which party true Christian unity has been lacking up to this point. In this way then certainly our churches may be brought again into the state of sweet and pleasant unity, as they were in 1530, when our Christian confession was delivered at Augsburg to Emperor Charles V in the highest degree of unity among the electors, princes, cities, and theologians whose confession it was.

If I am not at all mistaken, someone would like to say to me at this point: "There always was dissension and offense in the church, so no one will be able to correct the situation now." I certainly know that well, and the church historians provide sufficient proof. Mixed-up, unsettled minds can always be found. But that is no reason just to fold your hands in your lap, as some wrongly suggest, and let it go on as it has been and do nothing about it. The more the devil tries to destroy that unity, the more reason we have to work earnestly and diligently for it. We do not want to be devoured by one another, as St. Paul threatens.

Therefore I am ignoring whatever has taken place on all sides in the meantime and whatever vexations I have encountered. I am in no way losing heart for this task, nor will I let myself be discouraged from it, especially since I have had the opportunity to become well acquainted with the foremost churches and schools of the Augsburg Confession, all of which I have visited in recent years. I am also acquainted with the people involved, though not so much with those tainted by false, impure doctrine—but then their support is not so great, except among those whom they have taken in with false, unfounded arguments, which will have no permanence in the long run. When those who have been so deceived by them see and grasp how correctly and honestly this task was undertaken—only to further the divine truth, through which peace and God-pleasing unity were being sought—they, too, like all the others who love God's Word, will promote this salutary endeavor, I hope, according to the best of their ability and each one according to his own calling. Not only the earnest admonitions of Christ but also the present urgency of the situation should exhort and drive us to that.

Thus, for the purpose of eradicating all evil suspicion from this praiseworthy and highly necessary endeavor, I am obligated to defend not only the endeavor itself but also, in order to promote it further, I am obligated to defend all those who have advised, assisted, and joined in the endeavor publicly before all Christendom with a good, pure, unblemished conscience and with their testimony to the truth. I must defend them against all kinds of slander and obstacles. As I have said, this is intended to do nothing else than to honor God and to spread His holy Word in a Christian manner, against all idolatry, heresy, and all sorts of harmful falsification of pure doctrine, so that in so far as possible, protected against harmful scandals, the churches might again be brought into God-pleasing unity together. No reasonable, godly Christian who loves peace and divine truth, when he receives a true and complete report of the matter, will ever again criticize it.

Since the endeavor is not that of a man but of the Son of God, who told His mother at the wedding in Cana in Galilee: "My hour has not yet come" (John 2:4), we commend it also to Him with faith and prayer. With patience we await His hour, as Solomon taught (he testifies that everything has its time [Eccl. 3:1]). We have planted and watered (1 Cor. 3:6), that is, we have performed the service due to the Lord Christ in this task. He not only commanded us to carry it out, but before His last struggle He also prayed so earnestly to His Father, saying: "Holy Father, keep them in Your name, that they may be one as we are" (John 17:11). Therefore we will hope that He will give the increase so that the effort we have undertaken in the Lord is not in vain.

Even if it does not come to pass right away, it will finally find its hour. Everyone who has been given an accurate report on the basis of this endeavor, against the background of the present urgency, has not only favored the project but has also expressed appreciation for it to Your Princely Grace and to all who have pressed for it. They all have also promoted it and admonished me not to give it up until the end which we hope for has been accomplished, without regard for the gossip, insults, and ridicule which I have suffered or still may suffer in connection with the matter. I am still completely confident that the Lord will not have inspired this endeavor through His Holy Spirit without bringing great benefit and profit to the church. When you think that unity is furthest away, perhaps—hopefully—you will attain it very soon through His grace and wonderful providence at the time which He in His counsel has determined.

In the event, however, that it is not completely successful, the effort will nevertheless not be totally in vain. It will find its reward. And we will bring this testimony with us and have it at the glorious return of the Son of God, our Lord Jesus Christ, which He will proclaim to us with a glorious, new, unusual star from heaven, which has never been seen before, as a sign of the Son of Man. We will have that testimony as His dear children, brothers, and members who have sought godly peace in a genuine love of the truth. He certainly will reward all the humiliation suffered over this matter, richly, with eternal glory and splendor.

To Him I commend Your Princely Grace, together with your Christian, godly wife, and I also commend the young lords and ladies to His gracious protection. I commend myself obediently to Your Grace. Given at Tuebingen, Feb. 17, 1573.

Your obedient and willing servant,
Jakob Andreae

THE FIRST SERMON

On the Righteousness of Faith in God's Sight

Up to now we have dealt with articles of our Christian religion in which those who do not subscribe to the Augsburg Confession disagree with our churches, that is, the papists, Zwinglians, Schwenckfeldians, and Anabaptists.[8]

The theologians and teachers of the Augsburg Confession have parted ways over the proper and correct interpretation of certain other articles and have not presented the same teaching concerning them. So now we want to hear about these articles. They are (1) the righteousness of Christ, which is credited to us through faith; (2) the necessity of good works for salvation; (3) original sin; (4) free will; (5) ecclesiastical usages which are neither commanded nor forbidden by God and which are called adiaphora; (6) the proper function of the Law of God in the church; (7) the proper and correct distinction between Law and Gospel; (8) what the doctrine of the Gospel really is; (9) and finally, the person of Christ and the sharing of the properties of the divine and human natures in Christ. We want to deal with all of these, each one individually, as simply as possible, and to show the correct solution to the common layman from his simple Christian catechism.

This time we are talking only about the righteousness of Christ and what it means when we teach that it is credited to us as righteousness.[9]

Indeed, it has been proved more than sufficiently from the Scriptures of the prophets and apostles in the Old and New Testaments that the righteousness which avails in God's sight, which poor sinners have for comfort in their worst temptations, cannot and should not be sought in our own virtues or good works; nor will it be found there, as was proved above against the papists.[10] Instead, it should be sought only in Christ the Lord, whom God has made our righteousness and who saves all believing Christians and makes them righteous through knowledge of Him.

After this had been clearly proved, there arose a new dispute among some teachers of the Augsburg Confession over how this righteousness of Christ, which is credited to us through faith, is to be understood and explained. For when Christ or the righteousness of Christ is mentioned, there are three different things that can be understood by this word, "Christ": first, His divine nature and eternal divinity; second, His human nature, which He took upon Himself from Mary, the most praiseworthy virgin; third, His obedience, which He rendered His heavenly father unto death under the Law.

Since there are these different meanings—the divine nature, the human nature, the obedience He rendered His heavenly Father—the question is: Which of these three is credited to us through faith as righteousness? Holy Scripture, especially St. Paul, dealt with that question in detail and left the church its answer.

Here the one party set off and asserted that the righteousness of Christ ought to be understood as the eternal, essential righteousness of God, which Christ Himself is, as true God. It asserted that He dwells in the elect through faith and impels them to do what is right. None of their works could do that; it would have to be nothing else but God Himself. In comparison with His righteousness, the sins of all men are like a drop of water compared to the mighty ocean.[11]

The basis of this interpretation is this: This party looked first at the words of St. Paul, which he used in writing to the Romans: "The righteousness which avails in God's sight is revealed . . ." etc. (Rom. 1:17).[12]

This party asserted that that passage could really refer to nothing else but the essence of God and thus His essential righteousness, just as the goodness and mercy of God can refer to nothing else but God's nature and essence. In it there is not one thing that is His essence and another that is His righteousness, goodness, and mercy. Instead, such virtues in God are His divine essence itself. Therefore He is unchangeable; He does not change or alter Himself like a man. In man one thing is his essence, another his virtues. Even when he loses them, he is and still remains a real man.

Therefore this party taught that if a person has taken hold of the righteousness of Christ through faith, he is considered righteous in God's sight because of this righteousness, and God can cast him away no more than the Father could cast away His dear Son, Christ. For He has communion with the divine nature. What is God's nature? It is eternal truth, righteousness, wisdom, eternal life, peace, joy, blessedness, and whatever good can be mentioned. Whoever participates in God's nature receives all of this: He lives eternally and has eternal peace, joy, and blessedness; he is completely pure and righteous; and he is all-powerful against the devil, sin, and death.

They applied this interpretation to all the passages of the Old and New Testaments which speak of the righteousness of Christ, which is shared with and credited to believers.

They did this particularly with the passages of Jeremiah and Daniel: "At that time I will cause a righteous Branch to spring forth for David; and He shall be king and rule, and He shall execute justice and righteousness on earth. And this is the name by which He will be called: 'The LORD is our righteousness'" (Jer. 33:15-16).[13] From this they concluded the following: Here the great name of God, LORD, is used. That name can be attributed to no creature and is appropriate for neither human nature nor the work of man. This Lord is supposed to be our righteousness. Therefore this word "righteousness" can and must refer to nothing else but the eternal, natural, essential righteousness of Christ, the Son of God. This righteousness, which is Christ the Lord Himself, must dwell in believers, and because of it they are considered righteous.

The second passage is taken from the prophet Daniel, where the prophet wrote of the coming of Christ and pointed to the saving work He would perform for us on earth: "Seventy weeks are decreed concerning your people and your holy city, to finish the transgression, to put an end to sin, to atone for iniquity, to bring everlasting righteousness," etc. (Dan. 9:24).[14] So this party concluded from this passage: The eternal righteousness which the Messiah will bring is nothing else but the essential righteousness of the Son of God, our Lord Christ, who will dwell and remain in His elect eternally. Since He will be everything in them, He is their righteousness, which begins through His indwelling in us on earth, to be sure imperfectly. But it will be and remain perfect in the next life.

The third passage is taken from St. Paul's Epistle to the Corinthians, where St. Paul wrote: "Christ has been made our wisdom, our righteousness and sanctification and redemption by God, so that, as it is written, 'Let him who boasts, boast of the Lord'" (1 Cor. 1:30-31).[15] So, this party concluded from this, Christ has been made our righteousness, so that whoever boasts, boasts in the LORD; but the name LORD is the great name of God and must be understood as the divine essence. So it must follow that Christ is our righteousness only according to His divine nature and that its eternal, essential righteousness is reckoned to us through faith.

This party applied this interpretation to all the passages of the Old and New Testaments which speak of the righteousness of faith, especially those which mention the indwelling of Christ in our hearts: for example, Romans 3 (21, 25, 26): "Now the righteousness of God has been manifested apart from the Law . . . that He might show His righteousness . . . that He Himself is righteous and that He makes him righteous who has faith in Jesus"; likewise Romans 10 (3): "They did not recognize the righteousness of God and sought to establish their own righteousness and did not submit to God's righteousness"; 2 Corinthians 5 (21): "God made Him to be sin who knew no sin, so that in Him we might become the righteousness of God"; Psalm 71 (2, 15, 16, 24): "In Your righteousness deliver me . . . my mouth will tell of Your righteousness . . . I will praise Your righteousness alone . . . my tongue will talk of Your righteousness all the day long." [16] All these passages and many others as well were understood by this party as speaking of the essential righteousness of God and were applied to the righteousness of faith. St. Paul wrote about that to the Romans and in other of his epistles.

The other party held, taught, and wrote that the term "righteousness of God" in the doctrine of the righteousness of faith ought not be understood as the essential righteousness of God, which is God Himself and dwells in the elect through faith. Instead, it means nothing else than the forgiveness of sins for Christ's sake, for He is God and man and has fulfilled the law of God for us perfectly. If I may say it even more clearly, it means basically the obedience of Christ, which is credited to us through faith as righteousness, just as, by metonymy, faith in Christ is credited to us as righteousness. [17]

This party particularly insisted upon the proper and correct definition of the term "justification," as it is used by St. Paul in this matter, as it is used in Hebrew. There it means "to acquit" and to consider righteous or to absolve from unrighteousness and declare free, as it is written in Isaiah 5 (23): "Woe to those who acquit the guilty for the sake of money"; Proverbs 17 (15): "He who acquits the wicked and he who condemns the righteous are both an abomination to the Lord"; Psalm 51 (4): "so that You are considered righteous in Your sentence when You give judgment"; Job 9 (20): "If I want to justify myself, that is, consider myself righteous, He condemns me anyway." In such passages and more just like them the word "justify" or "be justified" means nothing else but "to consider and pronounce righteous, to be absolved from unrighteousness, that is, to be declared utterly free."

St. Paul used this meaning of the word "justify" in the Epistle to the Romans and in his other writings when he discussed the righteousness of faith: The justification of a poor sinner—his becoming justified—means nothing else but that he is declared utterly free of his sins, that he receives forgiveness of sins and is considered godly and righteous.

This can be seen particularly from St. Paul's use of terms since he sets the two words "justify" and "condemn" alongside each other, just as Solomon does. He wrote: "Who will bring any charge against God's elect? It is God who justifies; who is to condemn? It is Christ who died" (Rom. 8:33-34). So it is clear and obvious that the word "justify" means nothing else but to absolve, to declare utterly free from sin and therefore to consider righteous.

St. Paul shows with clear words what God looks at when a poor sinner is led before the judgment throne of God and is accused of his sins by the devil and his own conscience: He does not look at the poor sinner's righteousness, virtues, or good works, but instead He says, "Christ is here." That is, the heavenly Father looks at Christ. But what does He look at? His divine nature? His essential righteousness? No. Instead Paul says, "who died," etc. Paul included in that phrase all of Christ's obedience, which He rendered to the Father under the Law, even His most ignominious death on the cross. For that was the last and most difficult part of His obedience, suffering, and death.

Therefore, to speak properly, the Christian's righteousness on earth in God's sight, and thus the righteousness of faith, is nothing else but the forgiveness of sins, given out of the pure grace of God through faith because of the obedience of Christ, Son of God and of Mary. That obedience is credited to us as righteousness.

Everything St. Paul says is governed by this definition, not only what he wrote in the Epistle to the Romans but even to all other churches. For example, he writes: "For we hold that a man is justified through faith apart from the works of the Law" (Rom. 3:28); likewise, Romans 5 (18-19): "Just as through the disobedience of one man many became sinners, so through the obedience of one man many become righteous." How should that be understood when he says "through the obedience of one man," except that there are not two different things, our righteousness and His obedience, through which we obtain righteousness in God's sight. St. Paul explained that clearly to the Philippians (3:7-11), when he wrote: "Whatever gain I had, I counted as loss for the sake of Christ. Indeed, I count everything as loss because of the surpassing worth of knowing Christ Jesus, my Lord. For His sake I have considered all things as loss and regard them as refuse, in order that I may gain Christ and be found in Him, not having a righteousness of my own, based on Law, but that which is through faith in Christ, the righteousness which is credited by God to faith, that I may know Him and the power of His resurrection and may share His sufferings, becoming like Him in His death, that I may attain the resurrection from the dead."

Here Paul clearly explains the righteousness of faith and what it consists of: that God looks at His Son and for His sake permits us not to suffer for our sins; instead, He regards us as righteous, as if we were neither sinners nor corrupted by nature. He looks at the power of Christ's resurrection and our sharing of His suffering, for Christ's suffering and death are our death, and we become like Him through faith; we enjoy the power of His resurrection. Similarly he writes in Romans 4 (25): "He was put to death for our trespasses and was raised for our justification." That means: As soon as Christ rose from the dead, the power of His resurrection was so great that whoever believed on Him was no longer considered a sinner but was considered righteous in God's sight—for he had put on the obedience of Christ, which He rendered the Father even unto death. It is written (Gal. 3:27): "For as many of you as were baptized into Christ have put on Christ." Again (Col. 2:12-14): "You were buried with Him in Baptism, in which you were also raised with Him through faith, which God effects, God, who raised Him from the dead. And You, who were dead in sin, God made alive with Him, having forgiven us all our sins, having canceled the bond which stood against us."

From all this it is plain and clear that when Holy Scripture speaks of the righteousness of faith and of our justification in God's sight, nothing else can be understood but this: (1) how we are declared utterly free in God's sight of our sins, which we have committed, which still cling to our flesh, which we cannot completely lay aside as long as we live in this world; and (2) what God looks upon and why He will not regard us as sinners and does not cast us away and condemn us eternally as sinful, disobedient children: because of the obedience of Christ, which He rendered to His Father even unto death as the satisfaction and payment for our sins and as our righteousness.

St. Paul introduces the prophet David's witness concerning the forgiveness of sins when he speaks of our justification in God's sight (Rom. 4:6-8): "In this way also David says that salvation belongs only to the man to whom God credits righteousness apart from works, when he says, 'Blessed are those whose iniquities are forgiven and whose sins are covered. Blessed is the man against whom the Lord will not reckon his sin' " (Ps. 32:1-2). Here it is clearly shown that our righteousness in God's sight is nothing else than the forgiveness of sins, that God covers sin with the blood of His Son and does not reckon it as damnable. For to justify or to make righteous or to forgive unrighteousness, to cover sin, not to credit sin, all mean the same thing to St. Paul, and one can be taken and understood for the other.

Because Holy Scripture does not speak in just one way about this righteousness, but rather uses several different terms for it, different understandings of its meaning arose. The simple layman should recognize these.

For in the righteousness of faith three things always come together and are found alongside each other; none of them without the others justifies man in God's sight. First, there is the pure grace of God. Secondly, there is the obedience or merit of Christ; thirdly, faith. For where the grace of God the Father is not present, neither is the merit of Christ, nor faith. Again, when a person does not have Christ in His obedience, there is no hope of having the grace of God. Likewise, where there is no faith, neither the grace of God nor the obedience of Christ is of any use.

Therefore these three things belong together in the justification of the poor sinner in God's sight: God's grace, the obedience of Christ, and a true faith. For God is gracious only for the sake of Christ's obedience through faith.

These three elements are placed together when Christ says (John 3:16): "God so loved the world that He gave His only Son, that whoever believes in Him should not perish but have eternal life." Here Christ brought together all three: love, that is, the favor and grace of God; the obedience of Christ, His Son; and faith in Him. When all three elements are found together, the righteousness of faith, which is the forgiveness of sins, is to be found.

In the same way St. Paul also placed them together when he wrote (Rom. 3:22-25): "For there is no distinction; since all have sinned and fallen short of the glory which they should have before God, they became righteous without merit by grace through the redemption which has taken place through Christ Jesus, whom God has put forward as a throne of grace, through faith in His blood. This was to offer God's righteousness in which He forgives sins," etc. Here St. Paul presents explicitly the three elements set forth above: the grace of God, faith, and the blood of Christ, by which he understands Christ's obedience. He shows clearly that the righteousness which God offers is nothing else but the forgiveness of sins.

Sometimes, however, only one of these elements is mentioned, sometimes only two, but the others must be understood. St. Paul writes (Rom. 4:5): "Now to one who does not engross himself in works but believes on Him who justifies the ungodly, his faith is credited to him as righteousness." Here only faith is mentioned as that which is credited as righteousness. But it must be understood as including Christ, on whom he believes, and the grace of God by which we believe. Christ, too, said that the Holy Spirit would punish the world because of righteousness, for He was making His way to the Father (John 16:8-10); He mentioned only His "way," that is, His obedience, which was to be our righteousness. Of course, it is of benefit to no one without faith.

It is therefore good to note that the concept "obedience of Christ" is expressed in Holy Scripture in a number of ways. If the Christian reader did not remember this, he might get the idea that the Christian has many kinds of the righteousness of faith. For sometimes it is signified by the word "blood," Romans 3 (25): "Whom God has put forward as a throne of grace through faith in His blood," and 1 John 1 (7): "The blood of Jesus Christ, His Son, cleanses us from all sins." Sometimes it is signified by the word "way," John 16 (10): "For I make My way to the Father"; sometimes by the word "suffering," Philippians 3 (10); sometimes by the word "death," Colossians 2 (1:22). There are other similar words which are used to mean nothing else but His innocent obedience, which He rendered to the Father for us and as our redemption and justification.

"Yes," says the simple layman, "I hear that both parties attribute our righteousness in God's sight to the Lord Christ, but they have different interpretations. I hear, to be sure, that both parties cite Holy Scripture. Who will tell me which party speaks correctly or incorrectly about this matter? For I am a simple layman and can neither write nor read. Whom should I believe or follow?"

Here a simple layman should take the simple creed of the children and seek in it his righteousness. In this way he would soon see which party is correct and which is incorrect. For every simple Christian must seek his righteousness in God's sight only in his Christian faith; otherwise he would never find it. For in the Ten Commandments he finds righteousness which is difficult for him, which continually accuses him and condemns him. In the face of that righteousness he is never at rest until he finds and acquires the righteousness which is described in his Christian creed.

What does it say? There you recite: "I believe in the forgiveness of sins," that is: "I believe even if I am a poor sinner and should justly be condemned because of my sins, I do not doubt that God will not let me suffer for my sins but will forgive me by grace."

"Yes," says someone, "God is not only gracious but also righteous. He wants His commandments kept and will punish all transgressors." You answer: "He has punished them in His dear Son, on whom I believe. I confess what my Christian creed sets forth: 'I believe in Jesus Christ, His only Son, our Lord, who was conceived by the Holy Spirit, born of the Virgin Mary, suffered under Pontius Pilate, was crucified, dead, and buried,' etc. That has all taken place because of us poor sinners, not because of Him, who as the most holy one was not guilty and had no need of it. He was given to us, born for us, died for us, and rose again for our justification. That is, He has given us a witness with His resurrection and has decisively proved that through His obedience, suffering, and death He atoned completely for our sins and that we are justified by this, that is, we are made utterly free of these sins. I believe that and do not doubt it."

What should we say to the opinion and argument of the other party, which asserts that also the essential righteousness of God is ours and is in us, and that it impels us to do what is right, and if such an impulse from God is not in us, our faith is nothing.

To that the simple Christian should answer: "It is true that God is righteousness, as He is also wisdom and truth, Himself. It is also true that God, who is eternal righteousness Himself, dwells in the believers and elect as in His temple and sanctifies them and impels them to do what is right.

"But it is a completely different question and does not belong in this discussion if a person asks what God looks at in a poor sinner and for what reason He regards him as godly and righteous as if he had done nothing else but render perfect obedience to the Law with heart, thoughts, words, and works."

For the Father looks at His Son, and only at the obedience which He rendered for sinners. Because of this obedience He justifies the sinner from his sin, that is, He declares him free from his sins. After he receives this grace and obtains the forgiveness of his sin, not just Christ but also the Father and the Holy Spirit dwell in the poor sinner, regardless of the fact that in his nature sin remains (though it does not dominate him). They help him struggle against sin and begin to make him more godly and holy in his nature, until he comes to eternal, perfect righteousness. Daniel prophesied concerning this, that when faith and hope cease, we will not only be considered righteous but will be in fact and truth completely righteous and blessed in our nature and essence and will remain so eternally.

Actually, the one who began this controversy and defended this opinion did declare, on the other hand, that in the case of spiritual trials he pointed no one to the essential righteousness but only to the bitter sufferings and death of Christ, for comfort in the face of God's judgment.[18] Nonetheless, this phrase: "We are righteous in God's sight through the essential righteousness of God," is not used in Holy Scripture. From it arose this controversy, and it should not be used, in order to avert further offense and disunity and to maintain the pure doctrine of the righteousness of faith and to preserve the words of St. Paul in their correct and proper interpretation.

That is enough on the first article concerning which the theologians of the Augsburg Confession have quarreled with each other. Although it was a very scandalous controversy, nonetheless God, who lets nothing evil happen if He cannot make something good out of it, has produced this benefit for His church through the controversy: The chief article of our Christian faith, on which our salvation depends, has been made clear, so that there is not a passage in the Old or New Testament which has not been considered and discussed. Finally it was shown that the poor sinner is to seek righteousness neither in our virtues or works nor in the indwelling of the essential righteousness of God in us, but only in the obedience of our Lord Jesus Christ, which is reckoned to us as righteousness through faith. Only because of His obedience are our sins pardoned and forgiven. By God's grace this controversy has to such an extent died out that as far as I know there is no one left who is concerned about it or takes it upon himself to stir up the churches of God over it further.[19] Therefore we thank God for this and pray that the same thing may also take place in regard to the other controversies with which we want to deal in the following sermons. To God be praise, honor, and glory forever. Amen.

THE SECOND SERMON

On Good Works

About the same time as the scandalous dispute concerning the righteousness of faith arose, a controversy over certain formulations about good works took place among the theologians of the Augsburg Confession.[20]

One party expressed its opinion with the following words: "Good works are necessary for salvation, and it is impossible to be saved without good works," and: "It is impossible to be saved without good works."[21]

This way of speaking was considered scandalous and intolerable for two reasons above all:

First, it sounds contrary to the doctrine of justification through faith, on which salvation stands and falls. For St. Paul clearly states that we are righteous and saved only through faith, for the sake of Christ's merits alone, without any works, as is clearly seen in Paul's Epistle to the Romans.

Second, the dispute arose just at that time because the papists were pressing hard for a public confession on whether works are completely excluded from the righteousness of faith and whether this righteousness is credited to faith alone.[22]

Since this formulation made concessions to the papists, it not only obscured the article of faith concerning our justification but actually confirmed the accursed papistic error again, so that the people would stake their salvation, if not completely, at least in part on their own good works. That can in no way be tolerated or conceded.

The argument with which this party tried to prove that its formulation was alright is based above all on the passages which demand good works as the fruits of faith and its righteousness from the believers and the Christians who have been turned to God. For instance, Paul wrote: "If you confess with your lips . . . you will be saved" (Rom. 10:9). Now the confession of the name of Christ is necessary, but it is not therefore necessary for salvation. Likewise St. Paul wrote elsewhere: "If I have all faith, so as to remove mountains, but have not love, I am nothing" (1 Cor. 13:2). Therefore they say that good works have their reward in this and the future life, and therefore they are necessary for salvation.

Against that, the other party wrote that good works are not only not necessary but also harmful to salvation.[23] For salvation is not a work of our hands, that is, something we obtain through the merit of our works. Instead, it is only through the work of redemption, that is, through the merit of the most holy and innocent obedience of Christ, that it is obtained and earned.

Therefore when someone is arguing about salvation and how it is earned for us, all human work, no matter how holy it may be, ought to be set completely aside, as far as heaven is from the earth, so that Christ's honor may remain intact. He who bears the name Jesus will give His honor to no other, for the angel says: "He will save His people from their sins" (Matt. 1:21).

Thus Paul regards all his own righteousness as loss and refuse so he might gain Christ and be found not in his own righteousness but in the righteousness which is credited by God to faith, which consists in communion with Christ's suffering and in the power of Christ's resurrection (Phil. 3:8).

Therefore if a person is of the opinion that if he does works commanded by God he can hope to attain salvation through them, then such works are harmful for salvation as far as he is concerned. For he attributes to his own works what belongs to Christ alone, and that is sinful, unjust, and thus harmful as well.[24]

In this situation the common layman says: "How shall I make up my mind in this quarrel? For both parties cite Holy Scripture. And it is certainly necessary to present the doctrine of faith and good works at the same time and alongside each other, so that faith will not be understood as something dead and without good works."

Then he says: "In my opinion the so-called Epicurean faith, which does not devote itself to good works at all and which does not even admit that it wants to be saved, presents just as great a danger as does the hypocritical reliance on good works, through which the hypocrite hopes to obtain or earn salvation."

Therefore even a simple layman knows how to find his way through this controversy. He takes his old, simple Christian creed. In it alone and in nothing else he must seek his salvation and his righteousness before God. There he must see whether good works have a place in the creed. If he finds them in it, then they are certainly necessary for his salvation. If he does not find them in it, then they are certainly not necessary for salvation.

But, dear Christian, you will find there only the work of your dear Lord and Savior Jesus Christ and His innocent obedience, which He rendered to the Father on the cross and even into death.

This work alone—alone—alone—is necessary for your salvation, and without this work you cannot be saved; even if you had the good works of the whole world besides, it would not help you at all toward salvation. For when good works are performed without faith, they are sins in God's sight. Even when they are done out of faith, they are still imperfect and do not earn salvation of themselves. For they must be viewed with grace to be pleasing to God and not to be cast away along with the person who performs them.

Therefore in your Christian creed, where it deals with salvation, it says absolutely nothing about works but speaks only of the work of Christ, that He suffered under Pontius Pilate, was crucified, died, was buried, descended into hell. With that He obtained for you and all repentant sinners forgiveness of sins, that is, our righteousness in God's sight and eternal life, that is, our salvation. That is a simple answer.

Here a simple layman might say: "Both parties knew that only faith in Christ justifies and saves, and not a dead faith but a faith which is living through love. Why then is such a big thing made of using this formulation: 'Good works are necessary for salvation,' or the opposite formulation? For it was explained in a Christian way, that salvation is not attributed to our works and also that faith is not being taught as something dead and Epicurean."

The answer is that St. Paul earnestly enjoined and commanded his disciple Timothy to hold onto the pattern of sound doctrine diligently (2 Tim. 1:13). With this he not only demands sound doctrine but also sound words and formulations, which do not give rise to quarreling, controversy, or error.

Since this phrase: "Good works are necessary for salvation," cannot be found anywhere in the Holy Scriptures, but stinks like the accursed doctrine of the papacy, and since the people could be easily misled by such a phrase, it ought to be discarded in the church of God.

The phrase is not itself good German but rather Latin-German or Hebrew-German, that is, you just do not speak that way in the German language. For if the doctrine of good works is to be presented with its proper meaning, and if the people are to be scared away from sins as they are saved, then you should not say: "Good works are necessary for salvation." That is a papistic formulation. You should talk good German and scare people away from sin on the strength of God's Word: "You are bound for salvation not to curse, not to abuse the name of God, not to have contempt for God's Word, to honor your parents, not to get drunk, not to kill, not to commit adultery, not to steal, not to lie, and whatever more there is. But if you contaminate yourself with these vices, know that you have lost your faith, the Holy Spirit, eternal life, and salvation, and if you do not repent and refrain from them, you will finally not be saved."

That is the way to say it in German. It does not require much glossing when you threaten someone with the loss of his salvation. You make no concessions to the papists or to their accursed error with questionable formulations, which carry that error along in their knapsack.

The other formulation ought to be dealt with in the same way. It sounds no less scandalous and might give rise to an Epicurean life. For someone might say: "Good works are harmful for salvation," and out of that dream up that a Christian brings harm upon his salvation when he devotes himself to good works. This proposition is not found in St. Paul's epistles without any addition, just as it stands here. For when Paul said that he considers everything harmful (Phil. 3:8), he is making a comparison with "the surpassing worth of knowing my Lord Jesus." [25]

Therefore there is nothing more certain than that such offensive and dangerous formulations ought to be discarded, thrown out of the churches of God. We ought to stick with the sound words of Holy Scripture and discard a dangerous or offensive formulation rather than defend it with glosses. Instead, since that is not so dangerous, we ought to follow the admonition of St. Paul, who wrote of himself: "If food is a cause of my brother's falling, I will never eat meat, lest I cause my brother to fall" (1 Cor. 8:13). So when I see that someone takes offense at my formulation and I can present my ideas with other words, I will never again use this formulation.

Finally, since they were otherwise in agreement on the matter, they fell into a harmful quarrel over words, which as St. Paul says never benefits anyone (2 Tim. 2:14). For those who are listening are led astray, and it never benefits them but always offends and confuses them.

That is enough on this controversy over some formulations about good works and how you should use words carefully and plainly, not in a dangerous or equivocal way. Instead, remain with the edifying words of Holy Scripture and present pure doctrine with them. Other formulations should be discarded as offensive and harmful. In this way the church is edified, quarreling avoided, and pure doctrine maintained through God's grace without offensive quarreling. To God be praise, honor, and glory eternally. Amen.

THE THIRD SERMON

On the Controversy over Original Sin: What It Is, That We Are Corrupted in Our Human Nature Through It, and Whether Man Still Has a Free Will in Spiritual Matters

Dear friends, you have already heard about two articles concerning which some theologians of the Augsburg Confession have disputed with each other, and you have been shown which party is right or wrong and how a layman might decide and recognize this according to his simple Christian children's creed.

Now we want to hear something about the third controversy, concerning original sin, what it is, how far it extends, in what way human nature is corrupted in spiritual matters.[26]

From this controversy the dispute over the free will of man arose, over what the free will is able to do in spiritual and divine matters, especially in its conversion to God.[27]

Concerning original sin there are two opinions. One party has held, taught, and confessed that original sin is not something accidental [28] in human nature but that it is human nature itself, man's rational soul with all its powers, which after the fall of our first parents is the devil's creation and handiwork, opposed to the creation and handiwork of God, a spring and fountain of all the actual sins which man commits in thought, word, or deed.[29]

This party's argument is based on the passage of John (1 John 3:4) where he wrote: "Sin is wrong, or whatever is opposed to God's law." [30] From that they conclude, whatever is against God's law is sin; man's entire nature and essence, body and soul and all his powers, are opposed to God's law. Therefore it follows that man's nature and essence are sin itself and not something accidental in his nature and essence.

The one party's opinion rests entirely upon this one argument, and every passage of the Holy Scriptures which speaks of the corruption of human nature is drawn in to confirm it: wherever the corrupted man is compared with thorns and thistles, his heart with a hard rock, with a barren, decayed tree which has entirely lost its good essence.

The other party holds the opposite, that original sin is not man's nature, essence, or the rational soul itself, but it is something accidental in that nature. Thus there is the one entity—man, his nature or essence, or body and soul—which is completely different from the other entity—sin in man, in his nature, essence, body, soul, or all his powers.[31]

The basis of this party's opinion is this: God alone, and not the devil, is the creator of man's nature, essence, body, and soul. Furthermore, God is not a cause of sin. If original sin were man's essence (his body and soul), it would follow, since God has created man's essence (body and soul), that he also would be the creator and originator of sin, which is a horrible thing to hear.

Therefore there are two different entities: man composed of body and soul, and original sin. Sin is not man, his essence, his body or soul; but it is something in man's body and soul.

I want to explain that clearly with an example.

Adam, the first man, created by God, was himself in four dissimilar states. At the beginning, as he was created by God, he had no sin in him. Secondly, after the fall, he was a sinner and had sin in him. Thirdly, after he was received again by God to grace, he was at the same time a sinner and a righteous man. Then he still had sin in his nature, to be sure, but because of the woman's Seed (Gen. 3:15) it was not reckoned to him, and the Holy Spirit had begun to get rid of it, in part. Fourthly, he will again be completely without sin, cleansed from all sin, in the resurrection.[32]

Then comes the question: "Was the Adam who sinned a different Adam from the one who was created by God; was there one Adam who died and another Adam who will be raised from the dead because of Christ's righteousness?"

To that every simple Christian can answer: "There is just one Adam and not in essence two, three, or four different Adams. For the same Adam who was created is also a sinner and died, and the same one will rise in his essence."

This is the only difference: Adam before the fall was godly, without sin; but after the fall he is a sinner. Before the resurrection he is considered godly and is at the same time still sinful in body, soul, and all his powers. But after the resurrection he will be without sin, completely righteous and holy. For there is only one Adam in nature, substance, essence; there is not one soul which sins and another which does what is right.

From this it is plain and clear that sin is not the nature, substance, or essence of man. For man remains man in his substance, nature, and essence. He sins or he does not sin. There is only this difference. When he does not completely comply with God's commands or transgresses them, he is a sinful man. But when his nature does conform to them, he is a godly, holy man. Therefore original sin is one thing, and man's substance, nature, and essence is another thing. Original sin is not the nature and substance of man but a corruption of them, of man's mind, reason, will, and all the powers of his body and soul. They are corrupted in that they have no capabilities at all of themselves in spiritual things but are turned away from God, the highest good, to evil. Sin cannot exist in and of itself, but it is in the creation of God. If there were no creation of God, such as the devils and men, then there would be no sin. The devil and condemned men are and remain the creation of God, even after the fall. But sin in them is the devil's work. He got it started. He cannot create anything but can corrupt what was created good, with God's permission.

St. Paul demonstrates that with clear words when he writes: "I know that nothing good dwells within me, that is, in my flesh. For I do what I do not want to do; rather I do not do it, but the sin which dwells within me does it. So I find it to be a law that when I want to do right, evil sticks to me" (Rom. 7:17, 20-21). Here St. Paul clearly makes a difference between himself, that is between his essence, and sin. He does not say that he or his nature is sin but that sin is in him and sticks to him, that he desires to be utterly free from sin.

Therefore there is one St. Paul—his nature, substance, essence, body and soul—and something else, sin, which remains in St. Paul's substance, nature, essence, body and soul, and which sticks to him. He has his essence from God and his sin from the evil enemy, who attached it to our first parents.

So every simple layman can come to a decision on the basis of his simple children's catechism, where we confess: "I believe in God, the Father Almighty, Maker of heaven and earth," that is, of everything which is in heaven and on earth. From Him we have body and soul, eyes, ears, etc.[33] But we do not hear at this point that He created original sin.

It is said, however, that the nature of man is totally opposed to the law of God and it is therefore original sin itself.[34] That should be answered in the following way: The nature of man is opposed to the law of God only because of sin.

If it were not defiled by sin, it would not be opposed to the Law, as was the case before; before Adam sinned, his substance, nature, and essence were not opposed to God's law. Therefore there are two different things—man's essence, and sin. Neither is the other, although the one can be defiled by the other. Nothing but sin, and that which is defiled by sin, is opposed to the Law. Man's essence remains even though it is an impure, defiled, sinful essence.

That is enough on the first controversy and how a simple Christian should understand and make a decision about it.

The second question is: "In what way is man's nature corrupted through original sin, and what kind of powers have survived in it; to what extent do they remain, especially in spiritual matters, that is, in the conversion of man to God—may he still be capable of something, or of absolutely nothing, on his own?"

On this question there are again two opinions.

Some have held that although man has a corrupted and perverted will through the first fall of our parents (thus he is hereditarily corrupt from birth on), nonetheless he retains a very few powers from his initial created state. He does not have the ability on the basis of his own powers to restore himself, but when the Holy Spirit comes to him and assists and strengthens these powers which he has retained, then man has the ability through the power which is still his after the fall, since he still has a free will, to turn himself again to God—of course, with the help and aid of the Holy Spirit.[35]

For man is not a piece of wood or a stone, but even as an unregenerate man he has a rational soul, and thus he has reason and understanding. With them he can still differentiate good and evil to a certain extent. As the apostle testifies to the Romans concerning the unbelieving heathen, they still have a certain knowledge of God because of which they cannot excuse themselves before God. For he says: "They are without excuse. For they knew that God exists, but they have not praised Him as God" (Rom. 1:20-21). So this party says that man has in his will a hidden power. Thus he may turn himself to God. It is no different than a spark of fire which lies hidden in the ashes of a great fire. It cannot make itself into a fire, but when someone blows on it, it gets bigger and may become a big fire.[36]

All passages of Holy Scripture in which God accuses man of being unwilling are brought into accord with this interpretation, as Christ said of Jerusalem: "How often would I have gathered your children together as a hen gathers her brood under her wing, and you did not want to!" (Matt. 23:37). There not God's help and aid but man's will is accused of not wanting to. That would be a purposeless indictment if man could not will to turn himself to God.

Against this the other party says that concerning the free will in spiritual matters and in turning to God, there is nothing surviving except the mere term "free will." For the will of man is not only weakened but completely dead as far as doing good is concerned. It has no power or desire at all to do good; it has become an enemy of God and resists Him. Likewise reason, so far as true knowledge of God and His will is concerned, is not only weakened but completely corrupted and totally blind, as the apostle testifies: "The natural man," that is, he who has no more than a rational soul, "does not receive the gifts of the Spirit of God,

85

for they are folly to him. He is not able to understand them, for he must be spiritually reconstructed" (1 Cor. 2:14).[37]

Therefore man's heart is compared to a hard rock, which pays no attention at all to God and His Word until God makes a heart of pliable flesh out of it, as the Lord says through the prophet: "I will take the stony heart out of their flesh and give them a heart of flesh that they may walk in My ways" (Ezek. 11:19-20); and later: "A new heart I will give you, and a new spirit I will put within you; and I will take out of your flesh the heart of stone and give you a heart of flesh" (Ezek. 36:26). Thus David also prayed in the Psalm: "Create in me a new heart, O Lord, and grant me a new and steady spirit" (Ps. 51:10). If man still had a free will, so that he could turn himself to God, even weakly, on his own power, what need would there be for creating a new heart and transforming a stony heart into a heart of flesh? Instead, man's heart must remain what it is; only the Holy Spirit is able to grab him under the arm and help him.

Here again, the simple Christian says: "Which party should I follow? For they cite Holy Scripture for both positions, so I don't know what decision to make in this controversy."

He can easily come to a decision on the basis of his simple Christian creed, where it says: "I believe in the Holy Ghost, the holy Christian church." That means: "I believe that the Holy Spirit is the Third Person of the eternal divine essence, my Lord and God, and 'I believe that I cannot by my own reason or strength believe in Jesus Christ my Lord or come to Him, but the Holy Spirit has called me through the Gospel, enlightened me with His gifts, sanctified and kept me in the true faith, as He calls, gathers, enlightens, and sanctifies the whole Christian church on earth and keeps it with Jesus Christ in the one true faith.'"[38]

If then this all is the work of the Holy Spirit, then it is not the work of our reason or our will, which is not free but captive and even dead in regard to spiritual matters, as the apostle testifies. For he says that we were dead through sin (Eph. 2:1); he does not say half dead or simply weakened, but dead. Thus Christ also says: "Apart from Me you can do nothing" (John 15:5). That means that all human powers, whether great or small, have been completely reduced to the ground. Therefore man should not give himself the glory but rather give it to God alone, and say with David: "Know that the Lord is God! It is He that made us and not we ourselves. We are His people and the sheep of His pasture" (Ps. 100:3).

"That I cannot contradict," says the common layman. "But how will you reconcile the passages of Holy Scripture that are cited on both sides? Is the Holy Spirit speaking against Himself?" No.

Not every layman is able to do this; for prophecy, that is, the ability to give the proper explanation of Holy Scripture and to reconcile passages that appear to be contradictory, is a special gift of the Holy Spirit. Not everyone who can read the Holy Bible has this gift. Therefore a common layman should not venture into this and is not obligated to do so. For him it is enough to be able to give witness to the basis of his faith from his catechism.

So that we understand properly, however, that the Holy Spirit is not contradicting Himself and that the cited passages are not contradictory, you should note, dear friends, how God deals with a sinful man whom He wants to convert.

For God, when He acts according to His usual way of doing things, does not convert without means but uses the preaching of His Word for doing this. St. Paul says, Romans 10 (14): "How shall they believe in Him of whom they have never heard?" God could certainly give the Holy Spirit secretly without using preaching to whomever He wanted, but He has His way of doing things, and He lets us know about it. Therefore St. Paul says further: "So faith comes from what is heard and what is preached" (for they mean the same thing)—out of the hearing of God's Word.

So this is God's way of converting people to Himself: You first have to preach the Word of God. Second, someone must hear the preaching. Whoever does not go to hear the preaching does not hear it but despises it. He should never have the idea, as long as he continues to despise it in this way, that God will enlighten or convert him. Those who despise this Word of God can take no comfort in St. Paul, who did not despise God's Word but was a zealot on behalf of God's law, even though he was a persecutor of Christ and His church. Thus the Lord is not going to throw everyone to the dirt with a flash from heaven, as St. Paul was converted.

But even when someone preaches with zeal and others listen diligently, a man is not yet converted or believing. If something further is not added, he will never ever become a believer. The third factor goes along with it: God Himself, God the Father and His dear Son, Jesus Christ, together with the Holy Spirit. He grasps a man's heart in preaching and changes it. He makes a heart of flesh out of a stony heart and in this way creates a new heart. He alters his spirit and in this way creates a new spirit in the man who is to be converted. This is totally the work of the Holy Spirit, and man's power or ability has nothing to do with the Holy Spirit in this case. The honor belongs to God alone and not to the converted man. He is the potter or ceramics-maker, who forms the clay or dirt. The man himself does not; he is completely God's creation, and also in conversion he is a handiwork of God alone.

If you carefully differentiate the work of God and the means through which He works, you will find that the passages which have been cited are not contradictory but may be properly understood. Thus man is not a stick of wood or a block in his conversion but indeed much worse than a stick or a block.

For God accomplishes conversion through the preaching of the Holy Gospel, as shown above. This preaching must be heard with the ears on your head.

In regard to this instrument of the Holy Spirit, the preaching of God's Word, there is a great difference between a stick and a block and an unconverted man.

For man is a rational creature and can hear the Word, which a stick or block is not and cannot; for they are neither rational, nor can they hear.

And there is still a bit of the free will left in man after the fall, namely, that a man may go to church where the Word of God is preached, or he can stay away. He may listen, or he may plug his ears, as the high priests did in Acts 7 while Stephen preached.

Now our Lord God demands this obedience from those who are to be converted, that they go to church and hear the Word. When they do not do this, but despise the church, preaching, and the Word, they cannot say that God is guilty of their ruin if they are not converted. They themselves are guilty in that they despise the Holy Spirit, His means and instruments, and they will not permit themselves to find these, through which He effects conversion.

The words of Christ refer to this way in which God works: "Jerusalem, how often I would have gathered your children together, and you did not want to," that is: "You despised preaching, and you got rid of the prophets and apostles. You do not want to hear those through whom I gather My children and effect conversion with the power of My Holy Spirit. In this way you have obstructed your own salvation."

88

Even so it is also true, even when a preacher has preached a long time and the sinner has listened to him a long time, that the preacher is not so powerful that he can put understanding into the heart of the hearer; neither is the hearer so strong that he can grasp the preached Word through his own powers and believe it.

At this point the words of St. Paul fit, where he writes: "So it depends not upon man's will or exertion but upon God's mercy" (Rom. 9:16); and again: "I planted, Apollos watered, but God gave the growth. So neither he who plants nor he who waters is anything, but only God who gives the growth" (1 Cor. 3:6-7).

What that means is this: When someone has the determination and wants to be saved (and no one is so godless that he does not want to be saved); when he then pursues it, that is, strives for salvation and comes to hear the proclamation; when the preacher earnestly teaches, admonishes, rebukes, comforts him—even then there is not yet a conversion; it is not yet taking place. The human being is and remains forever according to his own nature and powers unconverted. Therefore human nature is absolutely nothing in its conversion and is capable of absolutely nothing for its conversion on the basis of its own powers. Of itself it must despair.

But when the third element [39] is added, the Holy Spirit, who gives the growth to preaching and hearing, then conversion takes place. It is neither the preacher's nor the hearer's accomplishment, for St. Paul says: "He who plants and waters amounts to nothing," and also: "It depends not upon the hearer's will or exertion," that is, he does nothing and is able to do nothing. Rather it is only the Holy Spirit's working. With His grace He changes man's heart, which man cannot change through his own powers. The Holy Spirit effects in him a new will and gives him a new spirit, which accepts the preached Word, believes it, throws its whole heart into it, and lives according to it.

The passages which the other party cites from Holy Scripture fit in here. They show that man's will is dead in regard to doing good, that his nature and essence is corrupted, that he cannot on his own either will or accomplish anything good, nor can he believe, in spiritual matters which concern our salvation. The passages of Holy Scripture cited above do not contradict this.

For when our will is accused of not having willed in Holy Scripture, this refers to the usual means of the Holy Spirit, to the holy ministry and to outward hearing and practices. It refers to godless taking of offense;

they do not want to put up with preachers and preaching, and so they despise the Holy Spirit, His means and instruments, through which He accomplishes conversion. They should not do that; they could do the opposite, and thus they are justly rebuked.

But when Holy Scripture speaks of man's corrupted character and nature and says that they are dead, blind in godly matters, inimical to God, and that they have become like hard rock, this is to be understood as referring to man's powers to understand the Word when he hears it, to accept it and believe it on the strength of his own powers, to say yes to it. This power is dead in us; it has been totally lost. It must be planted in us by the Holy Spirit alone. Otherwise there will never be a conversion.

This doctrine gives honor only to the Holy Spirit and the Lord Christ. With it no one has any cause to burst out with godless and angry words, as some say: "If I cannot on the strength of my own powers convert myself to God, then I want to live godlessly all the time. If God wants to convert me, it will happen; He does not want to do it, so I cannot force Him, for my will amounts to nothing."

No, that is not what it means. Instead, God says: "As I live, I have no pleasure in the death of the wicked, but that the wicked turn from his way and live" (Ezek. 33:11). From heaven He said of His Son: "Whoever hears Him," etc. (Luke 9:35). He preaches repentance and the forgiveness of sins. Hear that in the congregation which prays and makes supplication for you. In that congregation the Holy Spirit is present, and He makes the Word alive in the hearts of those who hear it.

Don't be confused by the fact that many hear and still do not believe and are not truly converted. You don't know how they are listening. St. Paul writes of them: "For such people seek to establish their own righteousness, and therefore they do not submit to God's righteousness" (Rom. 10:3).

In addition, the baptized all have this promise, that their lack of faith does not annul God's promise. Even when we denounce Him, he surely cannot renounce Himself; His hand is always outstretched.

Therefore no one should get the idea that because you cannot convert yourself to God, you therefore do not know whether God wants to convert you. Instead, you should do battle against this idea, which is a fiery arrow of the devil, with the shield of faith. You should say: "I know from the Word of God that God's will is not that I be damned." Therefore stick to His Word, and the grace and power of the Holy Spirit will not fail to remain with you; but it will be found in you for your conversion, improvement, life, and salvation.

That's enough on the third and fourth controversies among the theologians of the Augsburg Confession. The one is about original sin and what it really is. It is not man's rational soul, heart, nature, or essence itself, but something in man's soul, heart, nature, and essence: an abominable corruption of it. The result is that man's mind is clouded and in spiritual matters, concerning our salvation, he is totally blind. His will is perverted, and he has become an enemy of God. In the same way all inner and outward powers are corrupted, so that from the top of his head to the soles of his feet there is nothing healthy in man after the fall. Such corruption is inherited by all Adam's children.

The same holds for the free will of man in his conversion. In regard to outward elements and the Holy Spirit's instruments, he still has a free will, to go to church or to remain away from it, to hear the Word or to stop up his ears. For God demands an obedience which man can and should render.

But understanding the Word, grasping, accepting, believing, and saying yes to it—that is not within man's own powers, neither in part nor totally. It is instead the accomplishment of the Holy Spirit, who effects all these actions through the preached Word in the hearts of the elect. Whoever teaches otherwise does not understand what kind of an affliction original sin is in man. He takes honor away from God and ascribes it to the creature and leads godly hearts astray.

May the almighty God and Father of our Lord Jesus Christ grant us the grace of His Holy Spirit, that we recognize the greatness of our sins and our affliction, deplore them, and ascribe to ourselves nothing, but ascribe all honor to God the Lord, stick to His Word, in which we find grace, righteousness, life, and salvation. To God be praise, honor, and glory forever. Amen.

THE FOURTH SERMON

On Church Usages and Indifferent Things
Which Are Called Adiaphora:
How a Person Should Conduct Himself
in a Time That Calls for Confession in Regard to Them

The fifth controversy that arose among the theologians of the Augsburg Confession concerned things which are indifferent. They are called adiaphora; that is, they are things which God has neither commanded nor forbidden in the church. These may be observed or ignored as the church decides without harming consciences—except under coercion or at a time when confession of faith is necessary.[40]

This dispute took place at the time when Emperor Charles V wanted to impose upon the Evangelical churches not only papist church usages and ceremonies, which had long before fallen into disuse and had been abrogated through the doctrine of the Gospel, but also papist doctrine, except for a few articles.[41]

Different decisions were made after analysis of the problem. Some not only accepted the imperial declaration but also fully embraced the papacy once again.[42]

Some completely rejected and condemned the declaration as idolatrous and contrary to God's Word. Although it contained some good, it had been patched together to make the bad look good and to deceive the people.[43]

Some criticized the worst errors in it, but out of fear (to humor the devil and to deceive the emperor and others) they went halfway and acquiesced in some parts of the declaration, especially by restoring the ceremonies which had fallen into disuse. Some even worked it out so that the emperor and the papists were supposed to think that the declaration had been completely and fully enforced.[44]

Out of this a two-sided controversy developed. The one concerned the matter in itself: In a time when confession of the faith is required, can you—without harming your conscience—restore certain indifferent things (that is, ecclesiastical usages which had long before fallen into disuse and been abrogated) to please the enemies of the truth of God's Word?

One party held that that could and might well be done. For although it is not at all commendable in itself, nevertheless the dangers which arise at a specific time have to be considered. If this were not done, the churches would be deserted or handed over to the wolves, and the faithful servants of the church would be driven into misery with their poor orphans and children. On the other hand, if they would suffer this servitude, the churches might hold onto pure doctrine and their pastors, this party advised; such servitude should be suffered for a while until things got better.[45]

On the other side, the other party taught and zealously contended that at such a time and in such a situation you should neither accept nor yield on the least little thing to please the enemies of God's Word.[46]

For this matter arose not just over the surplice [47] and that sort of thing; it concerned an important article of our Christian religion, Christian freedom. Concerning it St. Paul contended very zealously against the false apostles and wrote against them to the Galatians: "Because of false brethren secretly brought in, who slipped in to spy out our freedom which we have in Christ Jesus, that they might bring us into bondage—to them we did not yield submission even for a moment, that the truth of the Gospel might be preserved for you" (Gal. 2:4-5).

So such hypocrisy, which in itself is a great sin, causes offense in two ways. It strengthens the enemies of God's Word in their error when they see that you begin to lean in their direction. For the pious it casts great doubt upon their true faith, as if they had done wrong to do away with the papist abomination. For the common people pay more attention to the external state of things than to doctrine and worship.

Therefore to preserve Christian freedom, so people would not be entrapped in the ordinances of men and so they would not eventually be led back into the damnable papist idolatry, you should not give a hairbreadth to the enemies of God's Word as long as they have not come around completely to pure doctrine and the complete worship and service of God.

Someone might say, however: "But with such servitude you can avoid a lot of trouble and in that way hold onto pure doctrine and preserve the churches which would otherwise be destroyed."

To that St. Paul answers: "You should not do evil so that good may come out of it" (Rom. 3:8). That is a miserable way to maintain pure doctrine, if you have to take such a course. For if the opposing party had succeeded in its intention and had gone ahead, the situation would not have remained like that. Instead the entire papist abomination would have had to follow, for this would have prepared the way for it.

However, this controversy did not arise over things which were just simply and purely indifferent but over much more abominable papist errors, peddled as adiaphora or indifferent things. They wanted to reintroduce these things in the churches again: the falsification of the doctrine of justification and of repentance; the demand for the seven sacraments; the distinction between the Mass and Communion; the establishment of papist bishops; the reception from them, the enemies of God's Word, of ordination; ecclesiastical laws against eating meat on certain days (which St. Paul calls the doctrine of the devil [1 Tim. 4:1-3]); and similar measures.[48]

Now comes the question: "What should the common layman decide on this issue and, if such a situation should ever develop again, how should he conduct himself without harming his conscience?"

The first question concerns purely indifferent matters, which in themselves are neither commanded nor forbidden by God. When someone wants to impose them upon him with force—and if he must suffer if he does not acquiesce—what should a layman do?

A layman should look at the Ten Commandments in his catechism and take to heart the First Commandment, which says: "I am the Lord your God," etc. "You shall have no other gods before Me." The Lord Himself has explained this commandment through Moses: "Everything that I command you, you shall be careful to do; you shall not add to it or take from it" (Deut. 12:32).

From that a layman can conclude that in His Word God has commanded us whatever is necessary; what He has not commanded is not necessary. When someone wants to impose something on me contrary to my freedom as a Christian, as something that has to be done, I have this command: I am not supposed to add anything to God's command or to take anything away from it either. Therefore just as he does wrong who wants to burden me with human commands through the use of force in his ardor, so I also do wrong when I offend someone else by letting myself be burdened.

Therefore even though what is being demanded of me may in itself be a free and indifferent thing (for example, I may or may not eat meat on a Friday or in Lent without harming my conscience), I neither can nor should tolerate it when in such a situation it is no longer free but becomes a command and an obligation. Then the truth of the holy Gospel stands or falls with the matter. In this case it makes no difference when it is said: "It was commanded by the authorities, not by the church."[49] For the authorities are paying court to the Antichrist, the pope, in that way. Therefore such deceit is to be severely censured.

This simple answer from God's First Commandment is very often set down and explained in Holy Scripture. Paul writes to the Galatians: "Stand fast therefore in the freedom for which Christ has set us free, and do not submit again to a yoke of slavery. Now I, Paul, say to you that if you receive circumcision, Christ will be of no advantage to you" (Gal. 5:1-2). And again: "Let no one make food or drink or specific festivals a matter of conscience for you" (Col. 2:16); and: "If you have died with Christ to the formulations of the world, why do you let yourself be captives of these formulations, as if you were still living in the world?" (Col. 2:20). And Christ said: "In vain do they worship Me, teaching as doctrines the precepts of men" (Matt. 15:9). And Elijah said: "How long will you go limping with two different opinions? If the Lord is God, follow Him; but if Baal, then follow him" (1 Kings 18:21).

The example of that glorious martyr Barlaam is appropriate here. His right hand was tied to the altar in such a way that he could turn it upside down but could not move it away from the altar. A fiery coal was laid upon his hand and incense upon it, and he let it burn through his hand rather than turn his hand upside down and sprinkle the incense on the idolatrous altar.[50]

For if dissimulation were alright, there would never again be any martyrs. Our Lord Christ wants our confession to be pure. "Whoever denies Me before men I also will deny before My Father who is in heaven," He said (Matt. 10:33).

Therefore, whoever has sinned out of human weakness in such a situation, let him confess it publicly before God and men. Let him be sorry and repent, for that is the first consequence of his sorrow. That often happened in the early church at the time of the great persecutions.

But when a person defends his action and claims to have done right, it serves no good purpose at all. You cannot remedy the matter in that way, but instead you arouse God's wrath so that He finally strikes such people with greater blindness. The result is then that, if they do not turn back, they finally lose Christ completely. Unfortunately, examples of this might be cited.[51]

Concerning those things which were not free and indifferent but in themselves gross and obvious errors, such as the papist extreme unction, the papist ordination, the papist confirmation, the papist Mass, parading the Sacrament on the day of Corpus Christi, and the like, there is no need to discuss them further. Instead every simple Christian should again consult the discussion in the first part of the sermons which I gave at Esslingen on the outstanding papist errors.[52]

For since we should flee and avoid the whole papacy and all its antichristian abominations, we should not accept them and introduce them again into the churches bit by bit, as it is written: "If anyone worships the beast and its image and receives a mark on his forehead or on his hand, he also shall drink the wine of God's wrath" (Rev. 14:9-10). And later: "Go out of her, my people, lest you take part in her sins, lest you share in her plagues, for her sins are heaped high as heaven, and God has remembered her iniquities" (Rev. 18:4-5).

This is enough on church usages and indifferent things, which are in themselves neither good nor evil, neither commanded nor forbidden by God—on what to do when they are imposed upon the church with force in a time which calls for confession of the faith, when they are a cause of offense for those who are weak in faith and strengthen the obstinate in their error, when accepting their imposition means the abrogation and diminution of Christian freedom. In such a case a Christian is in no way free to yield to the enemies of God's Word or to give in. Instead he is obligated to maintain his Christian freedom—and with it the truth of the holy Gospel—and to confess it publicly and to suffer whatever the Lord sends him because of it. The Lord certainly knows how to preserve pure doctrine and His church without such hypocrisy.

May the Almighty protect His dear church in these lands from that kind of affliction. But if He should permit it to happen again or if He should permit something more burdensome to develop, may He grant us the grace of His Holy Spirit that we may confess His Word and truth steadfastly in its purity and not play the hypocrite in the presence of His enemies but suffer with patience and overcome, so that we may be with Him, blessed forever. May the Almighty God and Father of our Lord Jesus Christ grant us that through His Holy Spirit.

THE FIFTH SERMON

On the Proper Distinction of Law and Gospel, and What the Gospel Really Is, and Whether the Law Should Be Taught to the Regenerate in Christendom

There was an old controversy in the church of the Augsburg Confession, soon after the Gospel was beginning to be revealed again, concerning the proper use of the law of God: whether the Law, that is, the Ten Commandments and God's reprimands and threats connected with it, ought to be proclaimed even to Christians.[53] At that time there was one man who asserted that Christians ought not be bothered with the Law. For the Law was given to the Jews, not to the Christians, who are righteous and do not need the Law. For it is written: "The Law is not laid down for the righteous" (1 Tim. 1:9). Christ also said: "The Law and the prophets prophesied until John" (Matt. 11:13). After him the Law and the prophets came to an end and therefore should not be preached among Christians.[54]

He insisted especially that Christians have been made utterly free from the Law. It had been a slave-driver, whose rod Christ broke. He won and gave the Holy Spirit to those who believe in Him. The Holy Spirit creates in them a freely willing spirit, which lives according to the will of God—not from compulsive force but from a free spirit.

So reprimanding sin could be done just as well—yes, even better—by the Gospel than by the Law. For the Law knows nothing about the greatest sin, not believing in Christ, and does not preach against it. For it is written: "The Holy Spirit will convince the world of sin because they do not believe in Me" (John 16:8-9). It does not say that the Law will convince the world.

Against that position Dr. Luther from the beginning and throughout his teaching held and taught that the Law, that is, the Ten Commandments, is a proclamation for all. This proclamation of the Law has been present in God's church ever since the beginning of the world, and it should be retained and earnestly proclaimed within Christendom to the end of the world.

For Christ the Lord Himself preached the Ten Commandments and presented and explained their proper interpretation against the false glosses of the Pharisees. He earnestly admonished all His hearers that they should live according to these commandments as according to the holy, righteous, unerring will of God. Read Matthew 5, 6, and 7.

The dear apostles did the same thing. They not only preached faith in Christ but also proclaimed repentance and the acknowledgment of sins. They also stressed living a Christian life in total dedication according to the guidelines of God's law. All their preaching of repentance, their reprimanding, and their admonitions to live a Christian life, particularly in the epistles of St. Paul, demonstrate this.

By its very nature the task of preaching demands and stipulates that, before you preach forgiveness of sins, you bring people to acknowledge their sins. St. Paul says clearly: "Through the Law comes the knowledge of sin" (Rom. 3:20). Therefore Christ, too, began His preaching with repentance and commanded His disciples to preach repentance and forgiveness of sins in His name.

Thus there are at all times, even in the midst of the church, people who need the preaching of repentance, since the devil causes one person today and another tomorrow to fall, one person in one way, another in another. If such people are to be restored again to God's grace, the Law must be preached first. From it they learn to recognize their fall and repent. This takes place in no other way except through the preaching of the Law. Through it hearts are brought low, and they are restored again through the preaching of the Gospel. It proclaims to them that Christ has fulfilled the Law for them and has made them utterly free from its curse.

A Christian can come to a decision on this controversy, too, from his simple catechism, and he can quickly see which party is right and which is wrong.

For among the Six Chief Parts of Christian doctrine, the Ten Commandments, the Christian creed, the Lord's Prayer, Holy Baptism, the Lord's Supper, and the Office of the Keys of heaven, he finds none which reprimand and point an accusing finger at sin except the Ten Commandments. They are the law of God, which says what is sin and what is not sin, what is right and what is wrong. They threaten those who transgress them with God's wrath and all sorts of punishment and torment.

Therefore either no sins should be reprimanded in Christendom, or the Ten Commandments must be preached just as much as the Holy Gospel.

"Yes," some say, "repentance can be preached and sin reproved just as well from the Gospel as from the Law, yes, even better than through the Law. For the chief sin and root of all sins is unbelief, not believing in Christ; and the Law knows nothing about that. Therefore Christ in the Gospel commanded that repentance and forgiveness of sins should be preached in His name" (Luke 24:47).

At this point a new controversy arose to renew the previous one, which had almost been buried. This one concerned what sort of proclamation the Gospel really is and represents.

The one party asserted that the Gospel really is a proclamation of repentance and a proclamation of the forgiveness of sins, together. To prove their opinion, they cited Christ's saying: "Christ had to suffer and on the third day rise from the dead, and repentance and forgiveness of sins should be preached in His name to all nations" (Luke 24:46-47). Here, they say, Christ clearly showed what the Gospel really is and means, a proclamation of repentance and a proclamation of the forgiveness of sins. In addition to this testimony of Christ they introduced other passages which strike the same note.[55]

Against them the other party asserted that the word "Gospel" is sometimes applied to the entire office of preaching and includes both Law and Gospel, which are to be preached according to Christ's command.[56]

But it is another question when Law and Gospel are compared to each other, as to what the Gospel means in its proper sense and in what way the two doctrines of Law and Gospel are distinguished. They answered: The Gospel in its proper sense is nothing else but a joyful, comforting proclamation of the forgiveness of sins for the sake of our Lord Jesus Christ alone, and in no way a proclamation of repentance. Through this latter kind of definition Law and Gospel are mixed together and the door is opened once again to the pope and his accursed doctrine.

For this is really the distinction between Law and Gospel: The Law teaches what sin is and points its accusing finger at us because of sin; it admonishes us to repent and teaches us how we should regulate our lives according to God's will.

On the other hand, the Gospel proclaims the forgiveness of sins, absolves from sin, and shows us the Mediator between God and man; because of Him we have forgiveness of sins and eternal life out of His pure grace. It is not because of our obedience which we have rendered to God with our own works.

In this sense Christ, too, said to His disciples: "Go into all the world and preach the Gospel to the whole creation. He who believes and is baptized will be saved, but he who does not believe will be condemned" (Mark 16:15-16). There the Gospel in its proper sense means nothing else than a joyous, happy message of the gracious forgiveness of sins. If we do not believe it, we commit a sin against God's first commandment; for Christ alone is its end and fulfillment (Rom. 10:4), and the Gospel points to Him.

It is very easy for a Christian layman to come to a decision on this controversy when he takes the sixth chief part of his Christian catechism, the Office of the Keys. It is used for the poor sinners whose hearts have been led to an acknowledgment of their sins through the preaching of the Ten Commandments and who have been terrified so that they fear God's wrath and want to have a gracious God who will remove the burden of their sin and take them up again into grace. In the law of God, however, they find no comfort or rest.

To them Christ has commanded that the Gospel be preached, that is, the joyous message be announced that He has come into this world for the sake of sinners, to save them, and that when they believe and are baptized in His name they will be saved.

The fact that the other party sticks to its position and wants to define the Gospel in its proper sense as not only a proclamation of the forgiveness of sins but also a proclamation of punishment and repentance is nothing but a brazen, dishonorable petulance. For they know well that they are wrong. They quarrel in such an arrogant way against the testimony of their own consciences; they quarrel so long over the Gospel that they are going to lose the epistles and even Christ Himself.[57]

For when they say that Christ has commanded the proclamation of repentance and the forgiveness of sins in His name, that much is true. He has not said, however, that the Gospel in its proper sense is a proclamation of repentance. Rather, as Christ Himself preached both Law and Gospel, so in the same way these two proclamations have always been presented alongside each other in the church of God from the beginning of the world on. Since one cannot save without the other, Christ wanted His disciples to present both alongside each other after His ascension.

It was, however, a clumsy move by the other party that it asserted in this controversy that not believing in Christ is not a sin against the Law, that the Law proclaims nothing about disbelief or belief in Christ. Certainly the end of the Law is Christ (Rom. 10:4), and there is not a different God in the Gospel than in the Law. There is one eternal God, who through the Law in the First Commandment demands faith and who gives it through the Gospel. Therefore St. Paul calls the Law a disciplinarian who leads to Christ. After it demands perfect obedience from us, and we cannot render it, it then points us to Christ, whose obedience is reckoned to us as righteousness and as the fulfillment of the Law.

Therefore you should know, dear friends, that on the one side there is nothing more than open petulance, which wrangles out of pure arrogance and pride. Although they see and understand the truth, they still teach this way. They can just figure that under the cover of this assertion the devil would like to introduce once more a burdensome obscuring of pure doctrine. For the proper distinction of Law and Gospel is not being maintained with all seriousness, as it broke into the open at the time when the Gospel was revealed. That distinction is to be regarded as a beautiful, glorious light, through which particularly the article on the justification of the poor sinner in God's sight through God's grace is maintained in its purity.

They were not even decent enough to God nor to His church, afflicted and torn as it is in so many ways, that they would free the church from this offensive controversy by testifying to the truth with just one word. If they would just say that they understand by the word "Gospel" the entire doctrine which Christ presented in both Law and Gospel (thus He preached both repentance, that is, the proper acknowledgment of sins, and also the forgiveness of sins), they would clear up this controversy.

If they do not want to do this, then the simple layman should not be deceived by their petulance, which will certainly be punished in time on this account and many others.

A third controversy arose over this article on the third use of the Law among those genuine, true, godly Christians who have been truly reborn and have been endowed with the Holy Spirit. Do they need the Law, too, as a standard and guide by which to govern their lives? Are they also to be motivated with reprimands and threats from the Law and to be kept in obedience in this way? [58]

The one party asserted that believers, enlightened Christians who are endowed with the Holy Spirit, do not need the Law, for they are righteous. No Law is given to the righteous man, for he does in and of himself what is righteous and needs no Law. He has the Holy Spirit, too; the Holy Spirit is a teacher of truth, who will teach and motivate him to do what he should do—the Law will not. Thus the ideas of Agricola were brought up again for discussion. They were dealt with in the first part of this sermon.

Against this party the other party taught that believers, justified and reborn Christians, need the Law.[59] From it they learn God's will each day and are concerned about conforming to it. For David, as one reborn, said that the man is saved who delights in the law of the Lord and meditates and walks in the Law day and night (Ps. 1:1-2). In Psalm 119, which speaks of the believer's life and behavior, the law of the Lord is stressed throughout: "Blessed are those whose way is blameless, who walk in the law of the Lord!" (v. 1); "Then I shall not be put to shame, having my eyes fixed on Your commandments alone" (v. 6); "I seek You with my whole heart; let me not wander from Your commands" (v. 10); "I have chosen the way of faithfulness, I set Your ordinances before me" (v. 30).

Here the simple layman says: "What shall I do in such a case? Both sides cite passages of Holy Scripture and both have a respectable claim to authority. So I don't know which I should follow."

Before I answer this question, I should show you, dear friends, in what sort of situation the justified believer is, as long as he lives on earth in this world.

As you heard, dear friends, in the previous sermons, particularly the first, about our justification in God's sight, the believers in this world are not righteous in such a way that they are perfectly regenerate and have no more sin in them. For sin clings to them their entire life. They have to fight against it until they die. The flesh always holds onto its desires, lusts, and inclination to sin. Thus the elect children of God never cease to carry their worst enemy in this world along with them in their hearts. Paul laments that in Romans 7 (vv. 18 and 23): "I know that nothing good dwells within me, that is in my flesh. The law in my members makes me captive to the law of sin, which is in my members."

Because "the desires of the flesh are opposed to the Spirit, and the desires of the Spirit are opposed to the flesh, to prevent you from doing what you want to," as St. Paul says (Gal. 5:17), the believer is in part regenerate but in part not regenerate. That gives us a proper decision in this dispute.

Insofar as the believer is reborn, he follows the Spirit of God, who is in him, as the standard and guide of righteousness and holiness. Insofar as he is not regenerate, the Holy Spirit uses the teaching and admonition of the law of the Lord. Christ does not free or absolve believers from obedience to it but rather receives them into grace so that they may henceforth live and act in obedience to God's commands.

For if man had not fallen and had never sinned, he would never have been without a law. Instead the Law, that is, the unchangeable will of God, would have been written in his heart, and he would have conformed to it in all his thoughts, words, and deeds.

So the words of St. Paul: "The Law is not laid down for the righteous" (1 Tim. 1:9), are not to be understood simply as they stand. For Adam was given a law in paradise, when he was still righteous and holy before the fall; otherwise, he would not have committed a transgression. Instead, St. Paul means that to those who are perfectly righteous there is no need for the compulsion of the Law because they do what they ought to do in and of themselves. It is instead necessary for the unrighteous, to hold them in obedience, as our entire nature is and remains in its essence an unrighteous, sinful nature right up until death. Therefore they need the Law so that they hear it daily, see it, and keep it in mind.

On this basis the fourth controversy which arose in connection with this article is also easily decided. One party contended that good works, although they are not necessary for salvation, are nevertheless necessary; that is, you are bound to do them, for creatures are bound to obey their Creator, as it is written: "We are debtors, not to the flesh, to live according to the flesh," etc. (Rom. 8:12).[60]

The other party contended that good works are not necessary but that they should be free, that is, they should be performed out of a free spirit, just as the sun runs its course not because it is compelled to do so but freely in and of itself. For David prayed for such a freely willing spirit, which conforms to God's commands with a free will, not because of compulsion, Psalm 51 (10). This party explained its opinion to the other party; it defined "necessary" as something coerced, so that good works would not be flowing out of a free spirit.[61]

This controversy has been considered no more than a dispute over words, a debate over the two words "necessary" and "free" and how they should be understood, since each party said the other did not understand and interpret its proposition correctly.

But when the matter is looked at carefully, it comes out somewhat differently; it does go right down to the doctrinal level.

For both parties are so learned that they surely understood each other, that the one party's opinion never was that it held that a Christian is free, or exists in his free will, so that when he wants and it pleases him, he does good works; when it doesn't please him, he may leave them aside and still remain and be a believing Christian anyway. For who would be so foolish and assert such an obviously gross error, particularly among learned, rational, and honorable people?

Instead, the opinion of that party was that it taught and held that good works flow and grow out of a genuine Christian faith, like fruit on a tree. Through this faith the heart is cleansed and the spirit is made free, so that you need neither the Law nor its threats nor its reprimands. Instead, it is all produced freely by God the Holy Spirit, as fruit is produced by the tree.

Therefore this party did not want to tolerate the word "necessary," by which it thought that this free, motivating power of the Holy Spirit would be obscured and easily be made into a coercion, contrary to the freedom of the children of God.

On the other hand, the other party did not understand the word "necessary" in the sense of such coercion at all, with the meaning that the good works do not originate from believers out of a free spirit that has been made free by the Son of God but must be tainted by force. Instead, this party understood the word "necessary" as God's order, that, as the holy apostle testifies, believers are created for good works, to live in them (Eph. 2:10). In that sense good works and incipient obedience are necessary, that is, according to God's order and will. That does not do away with the free spirit of believers at all, but it subjects them to the will and order of God even though they do them not because they are coerced but instead with a free will.

But every Christian can easily come to the conclusion, especially if he reads the first party's writings carefully, that there is an error hidden under its opinion when it expresses the idea that since believers have been made free by the Holy Spirit and do good works, they henceforth have no need for the motivating power of the Law nor for its threats and reprimands. That error was sufficiently refuted in the first part of this sermon, but this controversy gave it a new lease on life.

That would be a correct solution if, at the moment he is reborn, man were already in this world fashioned into what he will be after the resurrection of the dead—perfect, righteous, and godly—for then he will need no coercion. But with believers in this world it is set up in such a way that good works are performed not only according to the order which God has established (in such a way that they are necessary as the service owed to the Creator) but that good works are also performed both by a free spirit and by a spirit which is coerced. Insofar as man is regenerate, through the Spirit of God, he does what is good with a free will, not because he is coerced or compelled. For his will has in part been made free again. Insofar as he is not regenerate, however, and his corrupted nature is still clinging to him and he cannot get rid of it (St. Paul calls that "flesh"), there is pure coercion which must take his mind, reason, corrupted will, and all his hostile powers captive in obedience to Christ and subject them to our Lord God's wisdom and will.

We have two great examples of this in the two foremost apostles, St. Peter and St. Paul. For Christ said of St. Peter: "When you were younger, you girded yourself and walked where you wanted to. But when you are old, you will stretch out your hands and another will gird you and carry you where you do not want to go" (John 21:18). Now without doubt St. Peter willingly died for Christ's sake, but Christ nevertheless was telling the truth when He said: "He will carry you where you do not want to go." That should be understood as follows. According to the spirit and the inner man, insofar as he is regenerate, he was willing and had a desire to suffer for the Lord's sake. But according to his outward or natural man, insofar as he was not regenerate, he had neither the will nor the desire. For the old Adam, which clings to us until the grave, never has a desire to suffer but yields to it, flees from it, and grovels before it as long as he can.

St. Paul, too, writes of himself: "I pommel my body and subdue it, lest after preaching to others I myself should be disqualified" (1 Cor.

9:27). If his body, belonging to a regenerate man, had been willing of itself, it would not have needed to be overwhelmed with pommeling and subduing. To do that the Holy Spirit uses not only the Law and its stern threats but also very often stern punishments and afflictions. This can be seen in the case of David and other dear saints, so that they would not be condemned with the world, 1 Corinthians 11 (32).

Therefore when the one party says: "Believers need no coercion, no compulsion, no subduing; but all these things belong to the old ass, the old Adam, who is not yet regenerate," you just ask them again (no matter how holy they are) whether they do not still have a piece of that old ass skin or whether they have stripped it off completely.

If they say to you that they have taken it off completely, then they are more godly than any saint on earth has ever been, for the saints have all lamented over that old ass skin. The more godly they were, the more they lamented over it, as St. Paul, David, and other examples demonstrate.

If they say then, as they must, that they want to speak against the testimony of their hearts and consciences, and at the same time they want to be believers, then they have acknowledged their own error, reprimanded it, and condemned it. You can just let the matter rest there, and you have a really piercing analysis on the matter in reply to your question.

So, dear friends, you have in this sermon a simple analysis of four different disputes concerning the law of God, and you have learned how they should be decided according to the simple catechism.

From this it should be understood that these matters would not be so obscure in themselves if petulance did not accompany these disputes. For when the erring party has its error placed clearly before its eyes, it does not want to be so decent to God or His church as to yield to the other party and help restore Christian peace.

But that is nothing new; in the early church it happened many times. So godly Christians should not take offense at it but reap benefits from it. As stubborn and quarrelsome as such people are and remain, nevertheless the truth is not taken away but prevails evermore, as can be seen in this four-sided controversy on the law of God. The proclamation of the Law is a necessary proclamation in God's church and remains even among the elect, and the distinction of Law and Gospel must be maintained. This is demonstrated by the fact that the Gospel really is nothing else but a comforting, joyous proclamation of the forgiveness of sins for the sake of Christ's merits alone. It is only for those who hear it, whose hearts are terrified and brought to repentance and a proper acknowledgment of their sins through the proclamation of the Law; thus it is only for those who need such comfort.

This also clearly demonstrates that although the spirit of the believer has been made free by Christ's Spirit, so that it does what is good with a free will, nonetheless since his corrupted nature still clings to him and has not been swept away completely (and thus a continuous battle is still going on in the believers), they need not only the stern doctrine and admonitions but also the threats and reprimands of the Law. For God always holds His church under the cross because of the old Adam, to do him to death, until He makes things different for us in the future world, where we need neither Law nor Gospel nor epistle, but where we will serve the Lord forever in perfect righteousness with a free spirit and live with Him. To Him be praise, honor, and glory forever. Amen.

THE SIXTH SERMON

On the Person, Both Divine and Human Natures, and Also on the True Communion of the Properties and Majesty of Christ Our Only Savior

The tenth dispute among the theologians of the Augsburg Confession concerns the person of our Lord Jesus Christ on the following question: "Since in the person of Christ two natures, the divine and the human, come together and each nature has and retains its own properties, in what way are these two natures united and what does one nature communicate to the other?" [62]

This controversy did not originally begin among the theologians of the Augsburg Confession but originated at first in our times among the Zwinglians.

Zwingli began to teach that the body and blood of Christ are not truly present in the Holy Supper, but that the bread and wine only signify

107

the body and blood of Christ, which are not present. He taught this on the grounds that Christ retains His true body, in which He ascended into heaven, and therefore could not be present in the Holy Supper and at the same time be in heaven. As soon as he began to teach that, a debate arose because the body of Christ is indeed essentially like our bodies except for sin, but it is not just any old body but the body of the Son of God. Therefore there is a big and significant difference between flesh and the flesh of Christ. For the flesh is of no benefit, but Christ's flesh is beneficial.[63] For it has the life-giving Spirit who makes men alive. That raises the question: "What sort of majesty has the Son of God communicated to His human nature through the personal union?" For if He had been no more than Mary's son, He could not say truthfully: "I am with you always" (Matt. 28:20). No one else who had died could ever say that.

Zwingli quickly brought this term "alloeosis" into the discussion.[64] He asserted that passages which speak of the majesty of the Son of Man must not be understood the way they sound. Instead, when the Son of Man said: "I am with you always" and "No one has ascended into heaven but He who descended from heaven, the Son of Man who is in heaven" (Matt. 28:20; John 3:13), His words must be understood in such a way that one nature is taken and understood as representing the other, and He really meant: "My divine nature will always be with you."

Dr. Luther spoke out against this "alloeosis," which is a perversion of the magnificent passages on the presence of the whole Christ. With God's Word and the correct and proper explanation of the article of our Christian faith concerning the incarnation of the Son of God and His sitting at the right hand of the majesty of God, Luther showed that the person of our Lord Christ is divided and our Christian belief concerning Christ is falsified and perverted by this perverted interpretation of Zwingli's.[65]

After the controversy over the Lord's Supper got started again a number of years ago,[66] the new theologians at Wittenberg hid behind the bush for a long time and never expressed their opinion openly at all.[67] But through secret writings they let it be known that they were pointing their ears in a Zwinglian direction. When they saw their chance (as is typical of this kind of spirit, that it sneaks around in darkness), they came out with public writings and gave public support to the Zwinglians on this article concerning the majesty of the Son of God.[68] What Dr. Luther had

108

written against the Zwinglians, which had also been printed in Wittenberg and included in his books, was condemned and rejected as a Eutychian heresy.[69]

Of course, they did not use Dr. Luther's name.[70] For he still commanded great respect among many, also of their own people. They condemned and rejected his position under the names of those who had quoted and used Dr. Luther's teaching and writings against the Zwinglians. That way they would not give offense to people with a crude condemnation of Dr. Luther, their preceptor. They would wait until the Zwinglian error had made a better impression on the people, and then they might get rid of Dr. Luther completely without any fear.

This article was dealt with sufficiently in the sermons against the Zwinglians, and a simple layman can get a full analysis there and dismiss these new Zwinglians.[71] So it was probably unnecessary to present a special sermon about them; such fellows should simply have been brought forth along with the Zwinglians. Nonetheless, it is necessary because this error is being pushed and pedaled under the name of the Augsburg Confession, even though all those who teach and confess this statement of faith have always rejected and condemned it as no more than the basis of the Zwinglian error. A good deal of great importance is involved in this article, specifically our salvation as it is concerned with a correct knowledge of Jesus Christ. It is written: "This is eternal life, that they know You, the only true God, and Jesus Christ, whom You have sent" (John 17:3). Can you hear too much about Him? We want to present the entire matter as briefly and simply as possible, by God's grace so clearly and plainly that everyone who learned only the simple children's catechism can see and understand this present error.

First of all, both sides recognize that two natures, divine and human, come together in Christ.

Both sides also recognize and do not dispute that each nature has and retains its own properties and that they never become the properties of the other nature, nor could they do so.

The question is, however, whether the human nature in Christ, which retains its essence and properties, in fact, in reality, has a true communion with the divine nature in Christ and its properties or not.

That can be explained with an example. It is a property of the divine nature to be almighty, for God alone is almighty. Therefore it is His property. Then comes the question: "Since the almighty Son of God has assumed human nature into the unity of His person, what part of this omnipotence does the human nature in Christ have? Does Christ according to His human nature possess no more than the label 'almighty,' or does He have omnipotence itself; has He thus become almighty as the Son of Man?''

Here those theologians who want to be thought of as subscribing to the Augsburg Confession [72] say with the Zwinglians that Christ as Mary's son, that is according to His humanity, has in fact, in reality, nothing in common with the omnipotence of the Son of God. Or, to say it more clearly, the human nature really has nothing in common with the omnipotence of the divine nature except for the label—but in fact, in reality, absolutely nothing.

The basis of their opinion is this: Omnipotence is a property of the divine nature alone. The divine nature cannot be communicated to the human nature, for the divine nature is an infinite essence, and no creature is capable of having such an infinite essence, nor can it embrace that essence. Thus God's omnipotence is infinite, and if it is communicated to the human nature and the human nature holds it in common with the divine, then it would not be a property of the divine nature anymore. For what is common to two things is no longer the property of just the one.

Therefore the person of the Son of God is not supposed to be communicated to the assumed human nature or have anything in common with it. For just that is the property of one person, that it is incommunicable, that is, it cannot be communicated to another person.

From this they make the general conclusion that neither the divine nature nor the person of the Son of God, nor its properties, nor its majesty, nor its actions can be communicated to the human nature in Christ.

The Zwinglians drew this teaching into the matter concerning the Lord's Supper and asserted that among other properties of the divine essence is also the ability to be present in many or all places. This property could not be communicated to any creature; therefore it is also impossible that the body of Christ, which is a creature, could be present at the same time in heaven and on earth in the Holy Supper. Along this line they explained the secret of the personal union of both natures and the presence of Christ according to His human nature with several clumsy comparisons. It is like a precious jewel set in a golden ring. It is like a planet and the orbit in which it moves. It is like a tree with its nests.

110

It is like a man's head with its members. They asserted that, as it does not follow that wherever the orbit of the planet or the entire ring is, there the planet or the jewel in the ring is as well; so you cannot say that wherever the divine nature is, the human nature of Christ is also present. For the orbit of a planet extends further than the planet itself, and the ring encompasses more than the jewel which is in the ring. Likewise the divine nature encompasses more than the human nature of Christ, which is united with it in one place, at the present time with God in heaven, just as the jewel is not at all points in the ring but just in one place, where it is set in the ring. Therefore, they say, only the divine nature of Christ is present in the Holy Supper and His body is only signified with the bread of the Supper. This is the chief argument upon which the Zwinglians based their opinion right from the beginning.

But since the name "Zwinglian" was so detested, these theologians, who wanted to be thought of as men who subscribe to the Augsburg Confession, did not go so far out, but they asserted that they still held to the doctrine of the presence of the body and blood of Christ in the Holy Supper with Dr. Luther. But they publicly rejected and condemned the doctrine of the person of Christ which Luther presented and on which he based and proved his doctrine of the Holy Supper. For this doctrine demonstrates how God and man are one person in Christ and how His body can be in heaven and on earth at the same time.

In contrast to them, Dr. Luther believed, taught, confessed, wrote, and preached until He went to His grave that the divine and the human nature in Christ were united with each other, so that the Son of God truly and in fact communicated His divine nature and also its majesty to the human nature. Thus the apostle wrote that in Christ "all the fullness of the Godhead dwells bodily" (Col. 2:9), namely in the Son of God's own body. The fullness of the Godhead means and is everything that may be ascribed to God, all His omnipotence, wisdom, strength, and efficacy, as the apostle also wrote: "In Him are hid all the treasures of wisdom and knowledge" (Col. 2:3). Thus Christ as the Son of Man also said: "All power in heaven and on earth has been given to Me" (Matt. 28:18). Therefore also according to His human nature all things are subject to Him and cast under His feet, and He rules over them not as an absentee but with His presence (though of course not in an earthly, spatial way but in a divine-human way). *like 1 Cor 15*

So Christ has such authority and power that He is capable of more than a holy man is, since the Son of Man has in fact, in reality, been set at the right hand of the majesty and almighty power of God. He has absolutely no need of the accursed and condemned "alloeosis" of Zwingli. Thus you do not have to understand what is being said here in any other way than the way it sounds; that one nature should be taken for the other is not the way you have to understand these passages. Instead, since the divine and human natures are united personally in Christ, they have a true communion with each other. Likewise, since He has been set at the right hand of God according to His human nature, in which He suffered and humbled Himself, His human nature has been implanted into the divine majesty in fact, in reality. Therefore He is able and knows how to be present with His body in the Holy Supper. Thus His words can be understood according to the letter, according to the way they sound, and no other interpretation ought to be ascribed to them.

Dr. Brenz of blessed memory faithfully maintained this doctrine against the Zwinglians after Dr. Luther's blessed death, and because of this the Wittenbergers have accused him of being a Eutychian and a Marcionite,[73] as if he denied the human nature of Christ altogether because he, like Dr. Luther, steadfastly believed, taught, and wrote, and died in the belief, that the Son of God communicated all His divine majesty to the assumed human nature in His person. In his testament Brenz admonished as earnestly as possible that this doctrine of the majesty of the Son of Man never be deserted.[74]

Here the simple Christian says: "Which party should I follow? This question or dispute is over my head. I don't know how to get inside of it." No, my dear Christian, this question is not above your head, nor is it too complicated or too subtle. If you take your simple Christian creed in front of you, you can very easily figure out and grasp which party does not have the truth and is in heinous error.

For we confess in our simple Christian creed: "I believe in Jesus Christ, His only Son, our Lord, who was conceived by the Holy Spirit, born of the Virgin Mary, suffered under Pontius Pilate, was crucified, dead, and buried; he descended into hell; the third day He rose again from the dead; ascended into heaven; sits at the right hand of God the Father almighty. From thence He shall come to judge the quick and the dead."

If you just take these simple words, you will have the answer to this dispute at hand. For here you have just one Christ, not two Christs, one of whom is a God, the other the Son of Man; one from God, the other

112

born of Mary; one who suffered, the other who did not; the one risen from the dead, the other not risen; the one in majesty, the other not. Instead, there is a single Christ, Son of God and Mary.

From this we come to the simple conclusion, which can never be mistaken. No one is so simple that he cannot fathom this.

The Son of God is the Second Person in the Holy Trinity and possesses the divine nature in common with the Father and the Holy Spirit, and He also possesses all the properties of the divine nature, His omnipotence, infinite wisdom, power, etc. He assumes the human nature from the body of the blessed Virgin Mary. So the question is this: "What does He communicate to His human nature through this assumption, which is called the personal union?" The Wittenbergers (with words from the mouths of the Zwinglians) say that He does not communicate His divine nature nor its person to the human nature, nor its properties, omnipotence, infinite wisdom, powers, etc., as is shown above. They say that it cannot be, for it would transform the human nature into the divine.[75]

So you ask further: "If the Son of God, as far as His essence is concerned, possesses nothing except the divine nature, its person, and their properties, which make Him the only begotten Son of God and almighty, what has He really communicated to His human nature if it has nothing in common with the Son of God?" They answer that by saying that He has given His human nature greater power, greater wisdom, greater glory, greater majesty and glory than any other creature has. But in fact, in reality, He does not share in the omnipotence of God, which is a property of the Son of God. The same is true of all the other properties: His majesty, His power, His efficacy.

Now take the articles of the Christian creed at their simplest. Examine the creed in the light of this doctrine, and pay attention to what kind of a Christ you find there and what they finally make out of Christ.

Your Christian creed teaches you that the only begotten Son of God was conceived in Mary's womb for your sakes, born from her, suffered under Pontius Pilate, died, descended into hell, rose, etc.

Contrary to that, these theologians teach that the properties of His human nature were born, suffered, died, rose, etc., but that the Son of God has no real communion with the human nature, not according to His divine nature, nor according to His person, nor according to His properties, majesty, or efficacy. Because they assert that there is no true

113

communion in all these aspects, how can it be said truthfully that the only begotten Son of God was born from a human being for us, and suffered, and that we are redeemed through God's blood?

That is basically the heresy of Nestorius,[76] for he said: "Don't brag, you Jews, for you did not crucify God, but just a man." They say the same thing and use the phrase very much and very often; the human nature of Christ died for us. When someone says: "The Son of God died for us," it should not be understood as the words sound, but here one nature is taken for the other, they say. It means no more than that the human nature died for us and it is tied to or bound with the Son of God. But certainly it has no true communion with God's nature and its properties in Christ.

The same thing is supposedly true when the majesty of the crucified Christ is mentioned, that He has been set at the right hand of the majesty and power of God, which means that He is almighty and all power in heaven and on earth has been given to Him, that He has "ascended to highest heaven so that He might fill all things," as St. Paul says (Eph. 4:10).

On this the new Wittenbergers say, out of the Zwinglians' mouth: "That cannot be understood as the words sound," but they explain it through Zwingli's alloeosis and through the *communicatio idiomatum* [77] they invented. For them that is nothing more than an exchange of names, according to which the one nature is taken for the other. Thus the right hand of God is nothing else but the omnipotence of God, but omnipotence is an attribute of God, which cannot be communicated to any creature. Therefore even though Christ according to His human nature has more power than any angel or man, He nevertheless has nothing in common with God's omnipotence, nor does He possess any part of it. Thus He does not fill all things as a man, but only His divine nature does that. His human nature shares that nominally, *per phrasim* and *modum loquendi,*[78] that is, in a manner of speaking. It should not be understood as though as a man He in fact has true communion with this majesty.

Compare this doctrine and your simple creed, as you have believed all along at a very simple level, and then decide whether they agree with each other. If a person understands the matter correctly, it is then impossible not to say quickly: "Shame on you, Devil. Is that not a fine doctrine *de communicatione idiomatum,*[79] that is, of the communion of the properties of the divine and human natures in Christ, with which they put on a show and hide behind?" Yes, dear Christian, that's just it, and nothing else. Luther prophesied concerning this more than 30 years ago and repeated his prophecy shortly before his end: "I fear," he said, "that the devil is also among us (for who is among us more certainly than the devil?). For he knew that Christ is called a sacrament in the Scripture, as in 1 Timothy 3 (16), so he wanted to deduce from that that this is also a figurative expression when it is said, 'Christ is God and man.' He is not playing the fool for nothing." [80]

The new theologians at Wittenberg have fulfilled these prophecies with their *phrasi* and *modo loquendi* [81] when they say: "It is just a manner of speaking, but in fact, in reality, there is no communion." We will talk more of this at the end of this sermon.

Against this damnable doctrine the simple Christian says: "God forbids me into eternity to be persuaded to believe that Christ Jesus, Mary's Son, my flesh and blood, my Brother, is not truly almighty or that according to His human nature He has nothing more in common with the almighty power of God than the label, but in fact absolutely nothing. I believe firmly that He, as the eternal Son of God, is with the Father omnipotence itself, and that He has received this omnipotence according to His human nature. Therefore I believe that His divine and human natures are personally united in Christ. As the assumed humanity of the Son of God belongs to it, so also the Son of God with all the fullness of the Godhead belongs to the assumed humanity. Not just by label and title but in fact, in reality, they have this in common with each other in the person of Christ. Because of this real communion this all is ascribed to the body of Christ. That could never in any other case be by virtue of its own nature and essence except that it is the body of God's Son. Now if the human nature of Christ has no real communion with this essential property of God's Son in fact, how could His flesh be flesh that gives life, and how could I be fed with it in the Holy Supper? Likewise man's eye sees with a power which it does not have in and of itself, but which it has from a true communion with the soul. The teachers of the church have often explained this true communion of the two natures in Christ in this way through the simile of the body and the soul." [82]

From this a common, simple layman can conclude without contradiction that these new theologians, who still want to be considered loyal to the Augsburg Confession, are confirming the crude, open, and often-refuted error of the Zwinglians in public. To prove it they have

115

taken the passage of Christ: "The flesh is of no benefit; the spirit gives life" (John 6:63). From this they conclude that the flesh of Christ is not distributed in the Holy Supper, but only the spirit of Christ is present, and it gives life. This would certainly be true if the assertion of these new theologians were to stand when they write that the flesh of the Lord Christ has no true communion with the properties of the divine nature (which also gives life) and thus is not really life-giving flesh. Two hundred fathers at the Council of Ephesus held the opposite opinion and wrote that we participate in the body and blood of Christ in the Holy Supper, not as if it is the flesh of a sanctified man, but because it is the flesh which really gives life.[83] Whoever diminishes this communion of the properties of the Son of God is a Zwinglian and is presenting a damnable doctrine, which every Christian must flee, condemn, and curse into the abyss of hell as he would the devil himself.

"What do you say," says the common layman, "on the basic argument of the other side, when they assert that it cannot be since the divine nature is an infinite essence, which no creature is capable of holding and is likewise incapable of holding any of its properties?"

Here, my dear friends, you should notice what sort of crude, clumsy, fleshly concept these people have of the divine essence—as if it is a dimensional essence that is tall, long, wide. Along this line they compare the Godhead to an orbit of a planet or to a ring and the human nature of Christ to a planet or a jewel which is set in a ring. In this way they come to these crude concepts so that they cannot really believe the mystery of the incarnation of the Son of God.

There is another much different concept of the personal union of both natures in Christ. For the entire Godhead and all its fullness dwells in the human nature of Christ as in its own body, as it is written in Colossians 2 (9): "In Him dwells all the fullness of the Godhead as in its own body." The orbit is not inside the planet, nor the ring inside the jewel. Therefore all their ideas are false and nothing more than fleshly fancy, which cannot be compared to this mystery.

For if all the fullness of the Godhead can dwell in the man Christ, then the man Christ is also capable of holding it.

"Yes," they say, "the fullness of the Godhead dwells in Christ according to the divine nature but not in the human nature of Christ." We answer: "No teacher in all Christendom can be cited who has believed or taught that. For when the indwelling of God in Christ is

116

discussed, it was always understood in regard to His humanity, that the fullness of God dwells in Christ—Christ as a man or in His human nature—as in its own body." They have always understood the phrase in that way. That is good German, which everyone can grasp. These people dare not assert that there is no real communion with the fullness of the Godhead, and that means nothing else than His omnipotence, infinite wisdom, etc.

So we hold and believe that this kind of communion of the divine omnipotence with the human nature can in no way be separated from the divine essence of the Son of God so that the human nature has it in and of itself in its essence. For in that way two Christs would be created, if each person had omnipotence and power in and of itself. But, for example, in man there is only one soul, and whatever the human body does beyond what a body with no soul is capable of is all ascribed to the body because of the soul, with which it has a true communion. It also has a true communion with all its powers. Likewise in Christ there is just one omnipotence, the eternal, divine omnipotence, which belongs to the divine nature. The human nature shares it with the Godhead; for in fact, in reality, the Godhead and the humanity are one person in Christ.

Now it does not at all follow that if the Son of God shares His nature, His properties, His majesty, His efficacy with the human nature within the person (that is, in the way He assumed the human nature in the unity of His person), they are no longer His properties but that a mixture of the natures takes place. For the soul and its properties are not mixed with the body even if it shares them in the same way with the body. Body and soul are united so that the soul does nothing without the body, and the body is capable of nothing without the soul. The same is true of the properties of the Son of God forever. There is just as little chance that the Son of God can separate Himself from His assumed humanity as that He can use His omnipotence without His assumed humanity. They are personally united with each other, that is, in one person. This union cannot exist without the communion of His natures. The communion of properties follows directly from this. Thus the whole Christ is acting in heaven and on earth, and here neither nature is taken for the other, nor should it be taken or understood in that way.

From this brief explanation it is obvious what a dreadful error is hidden under this opinion, when it is asserted that the assumed human nature shares nothing with the Godhead and its omnipotence *realiter*,[84] that is, in fact, in reality. Through this all the articles of our simple Christian creed are perverted and falsified.

This is thus basically nothing else but the heresy of Nestorius, which openly made two Christs in two natures since neither shared anything with the other.

From this finally the Arian heresy resulted. It regarded Christ, the son of Mary, as a simple human being.[85] For through these theologians it is being stamped on people's minds that Christ, Mary's son, shares nothing according to his human nature with the divine nature, nor with the person, nor with the omnipotence, infinite wisdom, the power to make alive, etc. Instead, that is just a manner of speaking; that is, you can say it, but it is nothing more than a phrase; what can follow from that finally except that Mary's son is regarded as a simple human being? Out of the Nestorian heresy arose the Turkish, Mohammedan Koran, too, as Sergius had been a Nestorian and then helped fabricate this book, in which Christ's divinity is abused as greatly as possible and Christ is presented as simply a human being.[86]

Tragically, this has arisen again in our times, as Dr. Luther prophesied. Our Zwinglians struggled so long against the majesty of Mary's Son until some of them, and not the less important among them, finally denied His divinity completely and became Arians. You find examples of this in Poland, Siebenbuergen, and Heidelberg.[87]

Therefore I ask all Christians for God's sake to be on guard against this spirit with all diligence, for it clutches like Arianism and seeks to get the upper hand and would strangle all those who do not approve its accursed error and heresy, as examples demonstrate. Whoever does not want to be warned of this spirit and be frightened off from this accursed teaching, let him depart, for he willfully desires to be led astray and lost.

For myself, I testify before all Christendom that I have never approved this blasphemous, accursed error, which steals His omnipotence and all divine majesty from the Son of Mary, that is, Christ according to His human nature. That error leaves Him with only a label and title. By divine grace I never will approve this error, either. Instead, I want to warn all men of it, as of the very devil himself. For by his inspiration this spirit has been revived again.

On the contrary, I have admonished all sincere Christians that they remain with the simple articles of their Christian creed and not let themselves be separated from Christ. Rather they should hold onto Him

118

completely, God and man in His Word and in the holy sacraments, in every time of trial, since they may not understand the Lord's words in any other way than the way they sound, contrary to the Zwinglians' erring assertion. Instead they should believe simply this because as God He is omnipotence itself and as a true man has omnipotence, so that He may accomplish what the Word promises. Then they will truly have Christ and eternal life in Him.

So, my dear friends, you have heard a short, basic analysis of the 10 controversies which arose among a few churchmen and schoolteachers of the Augsburg Confession. Our enemy, the papists, have screamed loudly about this and asserted for reasons of their own (for their own gain) that you could not find among the churchmen of the Augsburg Confession two who agree on all the articles of the Augsburg Confession.[88] Thank God, the situation is much different. For some of these, particularly the first, have died out, and as far as I know no one holds that position anymore.[89] To a certain extent the others involve only a few people.[90] Except for them several thousand pastors are united on each and every article of the Augsburg Confession, and theirs is a true and steadfast unity, in no way just a painted-over unity. That will be made clear by God's grace at the right time with great rejoicing from many devout men.

Godly hearts should not become discouraged by these dissensions which we have just discussed, but they should instead be moved to make their confession concerning these matters and to remain steadfastly in this confession.

For in so many ways Satan himself has set himself against the Augsburg Confession, founded as it is completely on God's Word. He has done so not only through obvious enemies but also through false brothers (who cloak themselves with the name of the Augsburg Confession and want to push their own error under that cloak). As a well-advertised sign which is spoken against, as Simeon prophesied, this confession has remained until now unmoved and upright in its true and simple meaning as the unerring truth. Since it is founded upon the rock of God's Word, it has been able to endure all these storm winds easily. Finally the gates of hell, and the devil with all his false teaching, will not be able to accomplish anything against it, nor will they accomplish anything against it.

Therefore all devout hearts should earnestly call upon and pray to

Almighty God that He will preserve all of us unyielding in this confession. I hope to the Almighty that I shall be sufficiently well understood by all well-intentioned, devout Christians concerning the dissensions which have torn us apart in the churches of the Augsburg Confession. I hope they understand that I do not approve of any falsification of doctrine in words or in the essence of the matter, that much less am I covering up or spreading such falsification. I am eager to be open and candid at all times and give everyone an account of my teaching, faith, and confession, as often as necessary and it is fairly requested of me.

NOTES
Abbreviated Titles

Bekenntnisschriften	*Die Bekenntnisschriften der evangelisch-lutherischen Kirche*, 6th edition (Goettingen: Vandenhoeck & Ruprecht, 1967).
The Book of Concord	*The Book of Concord, The Confessions of the Evangelical Lutheran Church*, ed. Theodore G. Tappert (Philadelphia: Muhlenberg, 1959).
CR	Melanchthon, Philip, *Opera quae supersunt omnia, Corpus Reformatorum*, eds. C. G. Bretschneider and H. E. Bindseil (Halle and Braunschweig: Schwetschke, 1834—60).
WA	*Dr. Martin Luthers Werke* (Weimar: Boehlau, 1883—)

NOTES
Introduction

1. The following biographical sketch is based largely on Rosemarie Mueller-Streisand, "Theologie und Kirchenpolitik bei Jakob Andreae bis zum Jahre 1568," *Blaetter fuer Wuerttembergische Kirchengeschichte*, 60/61 (1960/1961), 224—395; see also H. Guersching, "Jakob Andreae und seine Zeit," ibid., 54 (1954), 123—56.

2. On Brenz's view see two studies by James M. Estes, "The Two Kingdoms and the State Church According to Johannes Brenz and an Anonymous Colleague," *Archiv fuer Reformationsgeschichte*, 61 (1970), 35—50, and "Johannes Brenz and the Problem of Ecclesiastical Discipline," *Church History*, 41 (1972), 464—79.

3. *Kurtzer vnd einfaeltiger Bericht von des Herren Nachtmal, und wie sich ein einfaeltiger Christ in die langwirige zwyspalt, so sich darueber erhebt, schicken soll* (Augsburg: Hans Gegler, 1557). Several other German editions and a Latin translation were subsequently published.

4. *Ein christenliche Predig vom Nachtmal des Herrn* (Tuebingen: Ulrich Morhart's widow, 1559), and *Bericht von der Einigkeit vnd Uneinigkeit der christlichen Augspurgischen Confessionsverwandten Theologen, &c. Wider den langen Lasszedel . . .* (Tuebingen: Ulrich Morhart's widow, 1560).

5. On the background and course of the Smalcaldic War see Franz Lau and Ernst Bizer, *A History of the Reformation in Germany to 1555*, trans. Brian A. Hardy (London: Black, 1969), pp. 157—207; its effect on Saxon religious life is discussed in Hildegard Jung, *Kurfuerst Moritz von Sachsen, Aufgabe und Hingabe* (Hagen, 1966), esp. pp. 104—67.

6. The text of the Interim is found in *Das Augsburger Interim von 1548*, ed. Joachim Mehlhausen (Neukirchen: Neukirchener Verlag, 1970), see Lau-Bizer, pp. 208—19, and Walther von Loewenich, "Das Interim von 1548," *Von Augustin zu Luther, Beitraege zur Kirchengeschichte* (Witten: Luther Verlag, 1959), pp. 391—406.

7. Lau-Bizer, pp. 213—15.

8. Gustav Bossert, *Das Interim in Wuerttemberg* (Halle: Verein fuer Reformationsgeschichte, 1895), pp. 15—16.

9. The text of the Leipzig Interim itself is printed in *CR*, VII, 258—64; see also cols. 48—62, 215—21. On the Leipzig Interim, see Emil Sehling, *Die Kirchengesetzgebung unter Moritz von Sachsen 1544—1549 und von Georg von Anhalt* (Leipzig: Deichert, 1899);

Johann Herrmann, "Augsburg—Leipzig—Passau (Das Leipziger Interim nach Akten des Landeshauptarchivs Dresden 1547—1552)," dissertation, University of Leipzig, 1962; and Luther D. Peterson, "The Philippist Theologians and the Interims of 1548: Soteriological, Ecclesiastical, and Liturgical Compromises and Controversies within German Lutheranism," dissertation, University of Wisconsin-Madison, 1974.

10. On Magdeburg's resistance to Charles V and Moritz see Oliver K. Olson, "Theology of Revolution: Magdeburg, 1550—1551," *The Sixteenth Century Journal*, III, 1 (1972), 56—79. On Flacius see the standard studies, Wilhelm Preger, *Matthias Flacius Illyricus und seine Zeit* (Erlangen: Blaesing, 1859—1861), and Mijo Mirkovic, *Matija Vlacic Ilirik* (Zagreb, 1960), as well as Henry Reimann, "Matthias Flacius Illyricus," *Concordia Theological Monthly*, XXXV (1964), 69—93. On his reaction to the Interims see Hans Christoph von Hase, *Die Gestalt der Kirche Luthers: Der Casus Confessionis im Kampf des Matthias Flacius gegen das Interim von 1548* (Goettingen: Vandenhoeck & Ruprecht, 1940).

11. On the disagreement of Amsdorf with Melanchthon's views on the freedom of the will see Robert Kolb, "Nikolaus von Amsdorf on Vessels of Wrath and Vessels of Mercy: A Lutheran's Doctrine of Double Predestination," *Harvard Theological Review*, forthcoming.

12. *CR*, VIII, 841.

13. *Das Doctor Pomer vnd Doctor Maior mit iren Adiaphoristen ergernis vnnd zurtrennung angericht Vnnd den Kirchen Christi vnueberwintlichen schaden gethan haben* (1551).

14. *Auff des Ehrenwirdigen Herren Niclas von Ambsdorff schrifft . . . wider Georgen Maior oeffentlich im Druck ausgegangen. Antwort Georg. Maior* (Wittenberg, 1552), lvs. Cv—Cijv. He laid out his position most completely in his *Ein Sermon von S. Pauli vnd aller Gottfuerchtigen menschen bekerung zu Gott* (1553). On the subsequent unfolding of the controversy see Robert Kolb, "Georg Major as Controversialist: Polemics in the Late Reformation," *Church History*, forthcoming.

15. Alvin H. Horst, "The Theology of Justus Menius," dissertation, Concordia Seminary, St. Louis, 1973.

16. Amsdorf first advanced his proposition in the preface of his edition of Luther's sermons on John 18—20, WA, 28, 766. He defended his proposition in a short tract, *Das die Propositio (Gute werck sind zur Seligkeit schedlich) ein rechte ware Christliche Propositio sey durch die heiligen Paulum vnd Lutherum gelert vnd geprediget* (1559).

17. *CR*, XXI, 375—76, cf. cols. 656—58; see Hartmut O. Guenther, "Die Entwicklung der Willenslehre Melanchthons in der Auseinandersetzung mit Luther und Erasmus," dissertation, University of Erlangen, 1963; and Michael Rogness, *Philip Melanchthon: Reformer Without Honor* (Minneapolis: Augsburg, 1969), esp. pp. 126—29.

18. *Demonstratio Manifesti Mendacii, Sycophanticus germanice editus titulo Nicolai ad Amsdorff . . .* (Wittenberg, 1558), esp. lvs. Br—Dr.

19. Amsdorf's *Offentliche Bekentnis der reinen lere des Euangelij Vnd Confutatio der jtzigen Schwermer* (Jena, 1558), lvs. (Div)r—Ev; Flacius' and Stolz's *Refutatio propositionum Pfeffingeri de Libero arbitrio* (1558). Pfeffinger replied with his *Nochmals gruendlicher, klarer warhafftiger Bericht vnd Bekentnis der bittern lautern Warheit reiner Lere . . .* (1559).

20. Flacius presented this position at Weimar according to his report of the disputation, *Disputatio de originali peccato et libero arbitrio* (1563); his defense of these concepts in his *Clavis Scripturae Sacrae* (Basel: Quecum, 1567), pp. 479—98, set off his dispute with Gnesio-Lutherans who had been his friends. On Flacius' position see Hans

122

Kropatscheck, "Das Problem theologischer Anthropologie auf dem Weimarer Gespraech von 1560 zwischen Matthias Flacius Illyricus und Viktorin Strigel," dissertation, University of Goettingen, 1943; Lauri Haikola, *Gesetz und Evangelium bei Matthias Flacius Illyricus* (Lund: Gleerup, 1952), esp. pp. 48—192. On Strigel's anthropology see Albert Pommerien, *Viktorin Strigels Lehre von dem Peccatum Originis* (Hannover, 1917).

21. Joachim Rogge, *Johann Agricolas Lutherverstaendnis, Unter besonderer Beruecksichtigung des Antinomismus* (Berlin: Evangelische Verlagsanstalt, 1960), esp. pp. 140—48.

22. Johann Seehawer, *Zur Lehre vom Brauch des Gesetzes und zur Geschichte des spaeteren Antinomismus* (Rostock: Boldt, 1887), pp. 18—58.

23. Christian Wilhelm Spiecker, *Lebensgeschichte des Andreas Musculus* (Frankfurt/Oder, 1858), esp. pp. 45—114.

24. Emanuel Hirsch's *Die Theologie des Andreas Osiander und ihre geschichtlichen Voraussetzungen* (Goettingen: Vandenhoeck & Ruprecht, 1919) must be corrected in the light of recent studies by Martin Stupperich, *Osiander in Preussen 1549—1552* (Berlin: de Gruyter, 1973), and Joerg Rainer Fligge, "Herzog Albrecht von Preussen und der Osiandrismus 1522—1568," dissertation, University of Bonn, 1972.

25. Martin Brecht, *Die fruehe Theologie des Johannes Brenz* (Tuebingen: Mohr, 1966), pp. 64—111; Otto Fricke, *Die Christologie des Johannes Brenz im Zusammenhang mit der Lehre vom Abendmahl und der Rechtfertigung* (Munich: Kaiser, 1927).

26. *Farrago confusanearum et inter se dissidentium Opinionum de coena Domini, ex Sacramentariorum libris congesta* (1552).

27. Melanchthon's memorandum is found in *CR*, IX, 960—66; Rogness reviews Melanchthon's view of the Sacrament from a different angle, pp. 129—35. On Hesshus in Heidelberg see Peter F. Baron, *Um Luthers Erbe, Studien und Texte zur Spaetreformation, Tilemann Heshusius (1527—1559)* (Witten: Luther Verlag, 1972), pp. 158—225.

28. *Bekanntnus und Bericht der Theologen und Kirchen-Diener im Fuerstenthum Wuertemberg, von der warhaftigen Gegenwaertigkeit des Leibs und Bluts Christi im heiligen Nachtmahl* (Tuebingen, 1560).

29. "Linde Fuerschlaege, dadurch man gottselige und nothwendige friedliche Vergleichung machen koennte zwischen den Wittenbergischen und Leipzigischen Theologen in causa Adiaphoristica und den andern, so wider sie geschrieben haben," reprinted from manuscript in Preger, II, 9—10; see his discussion of the document, pp. 8—13.

30. On the Coswig Colloquy see *CR*, IX, 23—72; on the Lower Saxon and Mecklenburg efforts see Preger, II, 41—62.

31. *Supplicatorii Libelli quorundam Christi ministrorum de synodo propter controversias gravissimas congreganda* (Oberursel, 1561).

32. The electoral Saxon summary of the colloquy is entitled *Acta colloquii Aldenburgensis, bona fide, absque omni adiectione* (Leipzig: Voegel, 1570); the Jena faculty offered its critique in their *Bericht vom Colloquio zu Altenburgk, Auf den endlichen Bericht* (Jena, 1570).

33. The text of the "Confession," a translation of which is found on pp. 58—60, is printed in Heinrich Heppe, *Geschichte des deutschen Protestantismus in den Jahren 1555—1581*, II (Marburg: Elwert, 1853), 250—54, and in Leonhart Hutter, *Concordia concors, De origine et progressu Formulae Concordiae ecclesiarum confessionis Augustanae liber unus* (Wittenberg:

Berger, 1614), lvs. 28—29. The following portion of this Introduction is found in substantially this form in Robert Kolb, "*Six Christian Sermons* on the Way to Lutheran Unity," *CTM*, XLIV (1973), 261—74.

34. Andreae reported on his travels in his *Gruendtlicher, warhafftiger und bestendiger Bericht: Von christlicher Einigkeit der Theologen und Predicanten, so sich in einhelligem, rechten, warhafftigem, und eigentlichem verstand, zu der Augspurgischen Confession, in Ober und Niedersachssen, sampt den oberlendischen und schwebischen Kirchen bekennen* (Wolfenbuettel: Horn, 1570), lvs. Aiijv—Fijv, and in letters printed in Christian Gotthold Neudecker, *Neue Beitraege zur Geschichte der Reformation*, II (Leipzig: Fleischer, 1841), 159—60, 170—72, 181—86, 189—201; see also Heppe, II, 257—72.

35. *Gruendtlicher Bericht*, lvs. Aiijv—Aiiijr; see also Heppe, II, 264—68.

36. Its text is given, ibid., II, 260—64, and in Hutter, lvs. 30—31.

37. Neudecker, II, 185, a letter dated Oct. 19, 1569.

38. *Bekentnis von fuenff streittigen Religions Artikeln, durch die Theologen zu Jhena gestellet* (Jena, 1570).

39. Neudecker, II, 204—10; cf. note 49.

40. Ibid., II, 241—42, in a letter dated April 1, 1570.

41. The *Corpus doctrinae Misnicum*, adopted as an official confession by electoral Saxony in 1566, was first published by the Leipzig printer Ernst Voegelin simply as a collection of Melanchthon's writings in 1560, *Corpus doctrinae Christianae, d. i. gantze Summa der rechten waren Christl. Lehre des hl. Evangelii . . . durch den ehrwuerdigen Herren Phil. Melanchthonen;* the Latin version appeared the same year. It included the three ecumenical creeds, the Augsburg Confession and its Apology, and six other doctrinal statements penned by Melanchthon.

42. Heppe, II, 301—11, used materials printed in Andreae's *Gruendtlicher Bericht*, lvs. Kijr—Liiijv, in Neudecker, II, 285—95, and a report by the electoral Saxon delegation in preparing its description of the Zerbst meeting.

43. *Gruendtlicher Bericht*, lvs. Liiijv—Nr.

44. "Swabian" Christology refers to that of Brenz and his colleagues in southwestern Germany, the area called "Swabia"; see note 25 for analyses of Brenz's understanding of the ubiquity of Christ's human nature.

45. Andreae's dissatisfaction with the "young Wittenbergers" is reflected in his letters to William of Hesse, July 27, 1570, and Sept. 30, 1570, in Neudecker, II, 319—20 and 330—34.

46. Ibid., II, 323—25, in a letter from August to William of Hesse, Aug. 4, 1570; August protested the publication of the "Recess" in another letter to William, Sept. 4, 1570, ibid., II, 327—29.

47. Andreae wrote William, May 20, 1570, ibid., II, 310—12, although he agreed in a letter of June 14 that the publication should be temporarily delayed, ibid., II, 313—15. He mentioned Duke Julius' support in a letter of Sept. 30, 1570, ibid., II, 331—34.

48. See note 34.

49. *Gruendtlicher Bericht*, lvs. Ar—(Fiv)r.

50. Ibid., lvs. Gv—(Giv)r, Hijr—Kijr.

51. Ibid., lvs. (Kiiij)v—Oiijr.

52. Neudecker, II, 358, a letter dated Feb. 19, 1571.

53. The slur word Philippists most often used for their Gnesio-Lutheran opponents. They used the term "Flacianist" because Flacius was one of the most prominent and outspoken of the Gnesio-Lutheran leaders and because he could be attacked as a foreigner, a "Wend" (a derogatory term for all Slavic people in 16th-century German).

54. Enclosure in a letter dated March 26, 1571, Neudecker, II, 364—66.

55. *Institutio religionis christianae continens explicationem locorum theologorum* . . . (1572).

56. *Drey und dreissig Predigten von den fuernembsten Spaltungen in der christlichen Religion, so sich zwischen den Baepstischen, Lutherischen, Zwinglischen, Schwenckfeldern, und Widerteuffern halten* . . . (Tuebingen: Ulrich Morhart's widow, 1568). Andreae stated that he was continuing these sermons in his *Sechs Christlicher Predig Von den Spaltungen so sich zwischen den Theologen Augspurgischer Confession von Anno 1548. biss auff diss 1573. Jar nach vnnd nach erhaben Wie sich ein einfaeltiger Pfarrer vnd gemeiner Christlicher Leye so dardurch moecht verergert sein worden auss seinem Catechismo darein schicken soll* (Tuebingen: Georg Gruppenbach, 1573), p. 1. It is impossible to determine whether the *Six Sermons* were actually preached, but the lack of dating and identification of place (present in his other published sermons) seems to argue against it.

57. E.g., in his *Ein Christliche Predigt von Christlicher Einigkeit der Theologen Augspurgischer Confession* (Wolfenbuettel: Horn, 1570), a sermon preached in Dresden March 22, 1570, he used the catechism to clinch arguments in behalf of his first and fifth articles in the "Confession," lvs. Diiijr and Gr; and he used the example of the martyr Barlaam in discussing the fourth article, lf. Fiijv, cf. Sermon Four, p. 92.

58. The ducal Saxons had attacked Andreae's person and work in their *Der Theologen zu Jena Bedenken und Erinnerung auf einen Vorschlag einer Conciliation in den streitigen Religionssachen* (Jena, 1569), and they criticized his "Confession" in the title mentioned in note 38. He replied in his *Sechs Predig,* p. 98, see this translation, p. 120.

59. Neudecker, II, 334, 349.

60. *Sechs Predig,* lvs. A2—A3v, see p. 63 of this translation.

61. *Christliche Predigt,* lvs. Giiijv—Hr; *Gruendtlicher Bericht,* lf. Qij.

62. *Sechs Predig,* lvs. B2—B3; see this translation, p. 65.

63. Hesshus had stated this view from the pulpit while Andreae visited Weimar in February 1570, Neudecker, II, 205. Eberhart von der Thann, secular counselor to John William of Saxony and an ardent supporter of the Gnesio-Lutheran theologians, echoed this view in his letter of Feb. 25, 1570, to William of Hesse, ibid., II, 213—14.

64. *Bericht von der Einigkeit vnd Vneinigkeit der christlichen Augspurgischen Confessionsverwandten Theologen, &c. Wider den langen Lasszedel* . . . (Tuebingen: Ulrich Morhart's widow, 1560); Andreae laid out his concern for the unity of the church also in *Gruendtlicher Bericht,* lvs. Piijr—Rijr.

65. *Sechs Predig,* pp. 97—98 and lf. B; see translation, pp. 64, 119.

66. Ibid., lf. B3r; translation, pp. 65—66.

67. Ibid., lf. A2r. In part his defense of the validity of his call and the sincerity of his effort was aimed at these Gnesio-Lutherans.

68. See Hans-Werner Gensichen's *We Condemn: How Luther and 16th-Century Lutheranism*

Condemned False Doctrine, trans. Herbert J. A. Bouman (St. Louis: Concordia, 1967), esp. pp. 123—52.

69. *Sechs Predig,* p. 77; translation, p. 108.

70. Ibid., pp. 3, 7; translation, pp. 68, 70.

71. Ibid., pp. 20—24; translation, pp. 77—81.

72. Ibid., p. 29; translation, p. 82.

73. Ibid., p. 30; translation, pp. 82—83.

74. Ibid., pp. 34, 36; translation, pp. 84—86.

75. Ibid., pp. 47—49; translation, pp. 92—93.

76. Ibid., pp. 59—60, 63; translation, pp. 99, 101. In the margin the Wittenbergers were accused of "wicked stubbornness" in refusing to agree with the other side that not believing in Christ is a sin against the Law.

77. Ibid., p. 77, translation, pp. 108—109. Andreae went on to describe how they condemned and rejected Luther's position while still praising his name, and the marginal comment labels this the "cunning of the new theologians at Wittenberg."

78. Ibid., lvs. A2v—A3r; translation, p. 62.

79. Ibid., lf. Br; translation, p. 64.

80. In 1574 Elector August dismissed a number of theologians and political counselors for political intrigue and Calvinistic theological leanings; he imprisoned a number of them. See Robert Calinich, *Kampf und Untergang des Melanchthonismus in Kursachsen in den Jahren 1570 bis 1574 und die Schicksale seiner vornehmsten Haeupter* (Leipzig: Brockhaus, 1866).

81. *Christliche Predigt,* esp. lvs. Bijr—Biiijr, Dr, Giiijv.

82. *Sechs Predig,* pp. 24—25; translation, pp. 79—80.

83. Ibid., pp. 94—95; translation, pp. 117—118.

84. On the issue on which Lower Saxons and Swabians had disagreed 20 years earlier, Osiandrism, Andreae went to great lengths to assure the readers of his first sermon that he supported the Saxon rejection of Osiander's position and did not share Brenz's early, mediating position; see Introduction, p. 36.

85. See note 3.

86. *Einfeltiger Bericht, wie ein jeder Christ antwurten soll auss seinem Catechismo, warumb er nicht mehr zu der Mess gehe* (Tuebingen: Ulrich Morhart, 1558).

87. *Drey und dreissig Predigten,* pp. 44—45 and 49—53; cf. *Sechs Predig,* pp. 38—39; translation, p. 87.

88. *Christliche Predigt,* lf. Ciiijr.

89. Andreae did not use the catechism of his friend Brenz in the *Sechs Predig.* He used the staples of the medieval catechism, the Creed and the Ten Commandments, with references to Luther's catechism at points. Although he abandoned use of the catechetical argument in subsequent efforts at creating the text of a formula of concord, e.g. in his "Swabian Concord" of 1574, Andreae did continue to use the catechism, including Luther's explanations to the chief parts, in sermonic analysis of the controversies which the Formula of Concord treats; see his *Ein Christliche Predig Vber das Euangelium auff den xxv. Sontag nach Trinitatis . . . Wie die eingefallene streitige*

Artickel vnter den Lehrern Augsp. Confession dieser Landen Christlich vergleichen/ Vnd ein jeder Leye/ aus seinem heiligen einfeltigen Kinder Catechismo gruendlich dieselbe vrtheilen/ vnd vor aller verfuerung moege bewaret werden. Gehalten zu Weymar/den 24. Nouemb. Anno 1577 (Leipzig: Steinman, 1578).

90. *Sechs Predig,* pp. 15—16; translation, p. 75.

91. Ibid., pp. 33, 37; translation, pp. 84, 86.

92. Ibid., pp. 51, 59, 61—62; translation, pp. 94, 98—100.

93. Ibid., pp. 38—39; translation, p. 87.

94. See the summary of the history of the Formula of Concord in *Bekenntnisschriften,* pp. XXXV—XXXVIII.

NOTES
Translations

1. The text of Andreae's "Confession" is printed in Heinrich Heppe, *Geschichte des deutschen Protestantismus in den Jahren 1555—1581,* II (Marburg: Elwert, 1853), 250—54, and in Leonhart Hutter, *Concordia Concors, De origine et progressu Formulae Concordiae ecclesiarum confessionis Augustanae liber unus* (Wittenberg: Berger, 1614), lvs. 28—29.

2. In a marginal note this party is identified as the "theologians in Thuringia, Mansfeld, and Regensburg," three centers of Gnesio-Lutheran influence.

3. This reference suggests that Andreae's loyalty to his friend Johann Brenz and to the latter's viewpoint became an important factor in his growing discomfort with the Wittenbergers, whom he had been wooing for his plan for establishing concord.

4. Although the margin provides no identifying note on this group at this point, the party referred to here is that of electoral Saxony, particularly the theological faculty at Wittenberg.

5. *Drey und dreissig Predigten von den fuernembsten Spaltungen in der christlichen Religion, so sich zwischen den Baepstischen, Lutherischen, Zwinglischen, Schwenckfeldern, und Widerteuffern halten . . .* (Tuebingen: Ulrich Morhart's widow, 1568).

6. Andreae identifies this party here with a marginal note, "the new theologians at Wittenberg."

7. Andreae's hopes were met the following year when Elector August of Saxony did remove the leading members of the party to which Andreae here refers from their posts in electoral Saxony on charges of "Crypto-Calvinism." See Introduction, note 80.

8. Andreae refers to his *Drey und dreissig Predigten* (1568). The *Sechs Predig* continued Andreae's work of analyzing differences between Christians and discussing solutions to these differences; the *Thirty-three Sermons* dealt with differences outside the Lutheran Churches, while the *Six Sermons* treated Lutheran disputes. See Introduction, pp. 48, 54.

9. The Formula of Concord deals with the righteousness of faith in its third article. See *Bekenntnisschriften,* Ep., pp. 781—86; SD, pp. 913—36; *The Book of Concord,* Ep., pp. 472—75; SD, pp. 539—51. On the Osiandrian controversy see Introduction, p. 34.

10. Andreae discussed the salvation of the sinner in sermons 4 through 10 of the *Drey und dreissig Predigten,* those dealing with faith, good works, and the assurance of salvation.

11. In the margin Andreae identifies this position as that of "Andreas Osiander." Osiander used this illustration in his *Von dem Einigen MITLER Jhesu Christo VND Rechtfertigung des Glaubens* (Koenigsberg: Lufft, 1551), lf. Yr. Andreae seems to have used this work of Osiander's as the source for his citations of Osiander's positions.

12. Osiander objected to Luther's translation of Rom. 1:17 as "the righteousness which avails before God" and insisted that this phrase be translated simply "the righteousness of God"; see *Von dem Einigen MITLER,* lf. Hiijv.

13. Osiander frequently used this passage as well as Jer. 23:6 in his writings; see *Von dem Einigen MITLER,* lf. (Qiv)v, *Bericht vnd Trostschrifft: an alle die: so durch das falsch, heimlich schreiben schreien vnd affterreden . . .* (Koenigsberg: Lufft, 1551), lf. Biijv, *Wider den Liecht fluechtigen Nacht-Raben . . .* (Koenigsberg: Lufft, 1552), lf. Cr.

14. Osiander cited this passage in *Von dem Einigen MITLER,* lvs. Siijv—(Siv)r.

15. Osiander cited this passage, ibid., lvs. (Niv)v—Or.

16. Osiander cited all four passages discussed in this paragraph, ibid., lf. (Siv).

17. Andreae identifies this party in the margin as "the theologians who subscribe to the Augsburg Confession, Dr. Moerlin, et al." On the opposition to Osiander see Introduction, p. 36.

18. Osiander did make this statement in *Von dem Einigen MITLER,* lf. (Biv)v.

19. With Osiander's death, Oct. 17, 1552, the controversy began to fade from public concern although Osiander's followers dominated the Prussian ecclesiastical scene until 1567; see Introduction, p. 35. Nonetheless, Osiandrism had to be treated in all the efforts at Lutheran unity during the following quarter century; both Gnesio-Lutherans and Philippists insisted on statements on the righteousness of faith.

20. The Formula of Concord deals with good works in its fourth article. See *Bekenntnisschriften,* Ep., pp. 789—90; SD, pp. 936—50; *The Book of Concord,* Ep., pp. 475—77; SD, pp. 551—58.

21. See Introduction, pp. 26—27. Andreae identifies this party in the margin as "D. Georgius Maior."

22. See Introduction, p. 21.

23. See Introduction, p. 27. Andreae identifies this position in the margin as that of "D. Nicolaus von Ambsdorff."

24. It was in this sense that Amsdorf advanced the proposition: "Good works are harmful to salvation."

25. Amsdorf used this passage in his *Das die Propositio (Gute werck sind zur Seligkeit schedlich) ein rechte ware Christliche Propositio sey/durch die heiligen Paulum vnd Lutherum gelert vnd geprediget* (1559), lf. Bv.

26. The Formula of Concord deals with original sin in its first article. See *Bekenntnisschriften,* Ep., pp. 770—76; SD, pp. 843—66; *The Book of Concord,* Ep., pp. 446—69; SD, pp. 508—19. On the controversy over original sin see Introduction, pp. 30—31.

27. Andreae reverses the actual chronological order of the controversies over free will and original sin in this sentence, since the former began in the 1550s and the latter in

the 1560s. The controversy over original sin resulted from statements made by Flacius in his attack on those who assigned some measure of responsibility to the human will in conversion; see Introduction, pp. 27—31. The Formula of Concord deals with free will in its second article. See *Bekenntnisschriften*, Ep., pp. 776—81; SD, pp. 866—912; *The Book of Concord*, Ep., pp. 469—72; SD, pp. 519—39.

28. As noted above, p. 30, the controversy over original sin began over the usage of the Aristotelian terms substance and accident; for Aristotle, substance is "that which underlies all outward manifestations; real, unchanging essence or nature of a thing; that in which qualities inhere, that which constitutes anything else." Accident is "a contingent circumstance, relation, quality."

29. Andreae's marginal note identifies this party as "Matthias Flacius Illyricus." See Introduction, p. 30.

30. Hans Kropatscheck, "Das Problem theologischer Anthropologie auf dem Weimarer Gespraech von 1560 zwischen Matthias Flacius Illyricus und Viktorin Strigel," unpublished dissertation, University of Goettingen, 1943, discusses Flacius' use of this passage, pp. 84—85.

31. Andreae identifies this party, in the marginal notation, as the Gnesio-Lutheran leaders Tilemann Hesshus and Johannes Wigand and others.

32. The schema of the four states of man was used in the discussion of the role of the free will in conversion by the representatives of ducal Saxony at the Altenburg Colloquium in 1568—69; Hesshus and Wigand were members of that delegation from Jena. See *Bekentnis Vom Freien Willen. So im Colloquio zu Altenburg/hat sollen vorbracht werden/von Fuerstlichen Sechsischen Theologen* (Jena, 1570), f. Aijv.

33. Andreae here quotes from Luther's Small Catechism, Article One of the Creed, *Bekenntnisschriften*, p. 510; *The Book of Concord*, p. 345.

34. In his *Clavis Scripturae Sacrae* (Basel: Paul Quecum, 1567) Flacius distinguished the material and the formal aspect of original sin. The material he defined as the perverse nature of man or the image of the devil; the formal as guilt and offense against God, I, 877.

35. Andreae notes in the margin that these included Viktorin Strigel and his followers. He omits any reference to Johannes Pfeffinger (see Introduction, pp. 27—28), which may be because Andreae had become personally involved in the controversy surrounding Strigel (see Introduction, pp. 30—31). Also, the Pfeffinger controversy was somewhat short-lived.

36. Although this illustration had been used a number of times by those associated with Strigel and the electoral Saxon faculties, Andreae may have been referring specifically to the use of the concept of a spark in man which is found in the reply of the theologians of Leipzig and Wittenberg to the Jena version of the Altenburg Colloquy, *Endlicher Bericht vnd Erklerung der Theologen beider Vniuersiteten/Leipzig vnd Wittemberg/ . . . Mit angehengter Christlicher Erinnerung vnd Warnung* (Wittenberg: Hans Lufft, 1571), f. 73v—75r.

37. Andreae identifies this party, in the marginal notation, as "Illyricus, Dr. Hesshus, Dr. Wigand, Nicolaus Gallus, and D. Musaeus."

38. Andreae here quotes from Luther's Small Catechism, Article Three of the Creed; *Bekenntnisschriften*, pp. 511—12; *The Book of Concord*, p. 345.

39. On the debate over the three causes of conversion see Introduction, p. 31. Andreae

here treats the problem in such a way that, while admitting a third cause, as did the Philippists, he meets the Gnesio-Lutheran objections to a third cause.

40. The Formula of Concord deals with church usages and the controversies discussed by Andreae in this sermon in its tenth article. See *Bekenntnisschriften,* Ep., pp. 813—916; SD, pp. 1053—63; *The Book of Concord,* Ep., pp. 492—94; SD, pp. 610—16.

41. See Introduction, pp. 19—21.

42. No prominent Evangelical theologians actually returned to Roman Catholicism at this time, but some pastors as well as many laymen submitted to the Spanish occupation troops and their German allies, whom Charles sent to enforce compliance with the Interim in many areas in southern Germany. For example, two pastors in the lands of Duke Ulrich of Wuerttemberg were persuaded to accept the Augsburg Interim; hundreds of others were sent into hiding or exile by the troops whom Charles had imported from his Iberian domains; see Gustav Bossert, *Das Interim in Wuerttemberg* (Halle: Verein fuer Reformationsgeschichte, 1895), esp. pp. 15—16.

43. See Introduction, p. 21.

44. Andreae here refers chiefly to the theologians in the employ of Moritz of Saxony; see Introduction, pp. 22—23.

45. In the margin Andreae identifies this position as that of "one part of the Wittenberg and papistic theologians." Melanchthon spoke of servitude and submission in matters not necessary for the confession of the truth in a letter to the believers in Frankfurt am Main, *CR,* VII, 324.

46. Andreae identifies this position as that of "Illyricus, Nico. Gallus, Hesshusus, Wigandus" and the Lower Saxon theologians in a marginal note; see Introduction, pp. 23—25.

47. The surplice became a symbol for the imposition of the ceremonies and trappings of the medieval church which had fallen into disuse in many areas of Saxony before 1548. According to the Leipzig Interim (*CR,* VII, 263; see col. 219), the "normal ecclesiastical vestments" were to be used in the celebration of the Mass in the Saxon churches. Against donning the surplice in compliance with the Leipzig Interim, Flacius and Gallus wrote their *Antwort auff den brieff etlicher Prediger in Meissen von der frage Ob sie lieber weichen denn den Chorrock anzihen sollen* (Magdeburg, 1550).

48. This list of errors was found by their Evangelical opponents in both the Augsburg and Leipzig Interims. The article on justification in the Leipzig Interim was criticized for omitting the word "alone" from its description of salvation by faith (*CR,* VII, 259—60; see cols. 51—59, 120—22). Even though the Leipzig Interim tried to change the meaning of confirmation and extreme unction, their restoration (*CR,* VII, 261—62; see col. 217) invited attack. The Leipzig Interim pledged obedience and subjection to the "highest and other bishops" as long as they exercised their episcopal office according to divine command; this its foes viewed as a surrender to the papacy although both Moritz's theologians and the Saxon lords who had acquired church property during the years of reform wanted no part of a full restoration of Roman ecclesiastical jurisdiction (*CR,* VII, 260—61). From such bishops, however, according to the Interim, Saxon pastors would receive ordination (*CR,* VII, 262—63). The Interim also enjoined abstaining from eating meat on Fridays and Saturdays and during Lent (*CR,* VII, 263—64). See Introduction, p. 22.

49. The Leipzig Interim stated that fasting was to be observed "as an external (i.e.,

130

nonreligious) regulation at the command of His Imperial Majesty'' (*CR,* VII, 263—64).

50. Andreae here relates the legendary account of the martyrdom of a peasant from Antioch in the fourth century; see *Butler's Lives of the Saints,* ed. and revised by Herbert Thurston and Donald Attwater, IV (London: Burns & Oates, 1956), 392.

51. Andreae here takes the Gnesio-Lutheran position; see Introduction, p. 27. Melanchthon admitted that he had taken the wrong position at that time (*CR,* VIII, 841), but he and his followers refused to perform the kind of public penance Flacius and his comrades demanded. See Hans-Werner Gensichen, *We Condemn: How Luther and 16th-Century Lutheranism Condemned False Doctrine,* trans. Herbert J. A. Bouman (St. Louis: Concordia, 1967), pp. 123—52.

52. See note 48 above. Andreae discussed the Mass and abuses connected with it in the 11th, 12th, and 13th sermons of *Drey und dreissig Predigten.* He dealt with confirmation, extreme unction, and ordination in the 14th sermon in the series.

53. The Formula of Concord deals with questions related to Law and Gospel in Articles V and VI. See *Bekenntnisschriften,* Ep., pp. 790—93 and 793—95; SD, pp. 951—61; 962—69; *The Book of Concord,* Ep., pp. 477—79 and 479—81; SD, pp. 558—63 and 563—68.

54. In this paragraph Andreae is presenting the controversy aroused by Johann Agricola; see Introduction, pp. 31—32. Andreae identifies Agricola in the margin at this point.

55. The controversy on the definition of the Gospel between Flacius and his colleagues on the one side and certain followers of Melanchthon, including Strigel, on the other is discussed above, p. 34. In the margin Andreae dates the controversy 1559, about the time at which Strigel and Flacius were disagreeing over the definition of the Gospel; he also specifically mentions the Wittenbergers and among them singles out Christoph Pezel, professor of theology.

56. Against defining the Gospel in the broad sense Andreae's marginal note ranges a number of Gnesio-Lutherans, including Flacius, Gallus, Hesshus, Wigand, and the theologians of Lower Saxony.

57. Note Andreae's play on words. His direct attack on the Wittenbergers in this and the following paragraphs is intensified by the marginal note on the fourth in this series of paragraphs; the note refers to the ''ornery petulance'' of the Wittenbergers.

58. In his marginal note Andreae identifies Andreas Musculus of Frankfurt an der Oder as the representative of the first party, which denied the use of the Law in the Christian life. On Musculus' dispute with Praetorius see Introduction, pp. 33—34.

59. Andreae identifies the second party in this dispute as Abdias Praetorius, Musculus' colleague in Frankfurt an der Oder, and Christoph Lasius, a Philippist pastor.

60. Andreae identifies this position as that of Praetorius in his dispute with Musculus.

61. This view is assigned to Musculus by the marginal note.

62. The Formula of Concord deals with the doctrine of the person of Christ in Article VIII; see *Bekenntnisschriften,* Ep. 804—12, SD, 1017—49; *The Book of Concord,* Ep., 486—92, SD, 591—610. The Formula deals with the related debate over the Lord's Supper in Article VII; see *Bekenntnisschriften,* Ep., 796—803, SD, 770—1017; *The Book of Concord,* Ep., 481—86, SD, 568—91.

63. Luther and Zwingli debated over the interpretation of John 6, particularly verse 63. The classic treatments of their debate are Hermann Sasse, *This Is My Body: Luther's Contention for the Real Presence in the Sacrament of the Altar* (Minneapolis: Augsburg, 1959),

esp. pp. 134—86; and Walther Koehler, *Zwingli und Luther: Ihr Streit ueber das Abendmahl nach seinen politischen und religioesen Beziehungen* (Leipzig: Eger & Sievers, 1924), esp. I, 462—562.

64. Zwingli used the figure of speech "alloeosis," the attribution of the qualities of one nature to the other, to explain away Biblical passages which seem to attribute divine qualities to the human nature of Christ.

65. Andreae speaks here particularly of Luther's *Sermon von dem Sakrament des Leibes und Blutes Christi wider die Schwarmgeister,* WA, 19, (474) 482—523; *Dass diese Worte Christi (Das ist mein Leib etc.) noch fest stehen wider die Schwarmgeister,* WA, 23, (38) 64—283; and *Vom Abendmahl Christi, Bekenntnis,* WA, 26, (241) 261—509. These works were composed in 1526, 1527, and 1528 respectively, at the height of the debate preceding the Marburg Colloquy.

66. Andreae refers here to the renewed debate over the Lord's Supper which was begun by Joachim Westphal's *Farrago,* his attack against Calvin's doctrine of the Lord's Supper. Andreae is probably thinking also of other debates with Calvinists in the 1550s and 1560s, including those of Tilemann Hesshus with Reformed theologians in Heidelberg and Bremen. See Introduction, pp. 37—38. In the margin here Andreae wrote: "The new theologians at Wittenberg have given public support to the Zwinglians."

67. The theological faculty at Wittenberg, under Melanchthon's leadership until his death in 1560, did not enter into the debate with Zurich and Geneva at all. Although Andreae and his fellow Wuerttembergers had tried accommodation, they had fallen into dispute with their Reformed neighbors to the south as well as with those in the Palatinate; see above, p. 38.

68. Andreae refers here to the documents of 1571 in which the Wittenbergers expressed their sacramental doctrine, including the *Wittenberg Catechism* and the *Dresden Consensus;* see Introduction note 80 for further references.

69. Eutyches, an early-fifth-century monk at Constantinople, has given his name to a heresy which denies that the manhood of Christ is consubstantial with the humanity of human beings, and on that basis asserts a monophysite view that there is only one nature in Christ after the union of His divine and human natures, the human nature being absorbed by the divine. See J. N. D. Kelly, *Early Christian Doctrines* (New York: Harper & Row, 1960), pp. 331—34.

70. In the margin at this point Andreae comments: "The deceitfulness of the Wittenbergers."

71. Andreae discussed Zwinglianism in three sermons in his *Drey und dreissig Predigten:* 1. (Aug. 3, 1567) the subject of the dispute, the basic arguments of the Zwinglians on the majesty of the man Christ; 2. (Aug. 10, 1567) arguments against the Zwinglian argument; 3. (Aug. 17, 1567) John 6, the distinction between eating the flesh of Christ in the Old Testament sense and the New Testament sense, what the unrepentant and godless receive in the Sacrament.

72. The Wittenberg faculty of course subscribed to the Augsburg Confession and believed it was presenting the developing theology of its author, Melanchthon. Andreae was countering that stance at this point, not only in the text but also with marginal comments alongside this paragraph and the following one. These comments linked the Wittenbergers with the Reformed theologians at Heidelberg and the Zwinglians.

73. Marcion (d. c. 160) taught that the Lord's body was phantasmal and that He was really the highest God (God the Father) clothed in the outward appearance of man. After the Maulbronn Colloquy of 1564 the Wittenberg faculty issued a *Censura Theologorum de disputatione Johannes Brentii et Jacobi Andreae de Maiestate Christi*, to which Andreae is probably referring here.

74. Brenz composed his testament in 1566, the first half of which dealt with his legacy to the church, his doctrinal position. It was published at Tuebingen in 1570 with the title, *Der erste Theil des Testaments Herrn J. Brentii, betreffendt sein Confession und Predigampt.*

75. Andreae, in a marginal note, labels this "the belief about Christ of the new theologians of Wittenberg."

76. Nestorius (d. c. 451) is said to have taught that the divine and human natures were completely separate and distinct. His holding to the complete distinction between the divine and human in Christ led him to reject the term "bearer of God," which the Council of Ephesus applied to the Virgin Mary. See Kelly, pp. 310—17. The marginal note here reads: "The new theologians of Wittenberg are clearly Nestorians."

77. Andreae here used the Latin phrase, which means "the exchange of properties" between the two natures of Christ.

78. Andreae uses the Latin phrase at this point and then translates it into German for his readers in the next words.

79. Andreae uses the Latin here for "concerning the exchange of properties."

80. In the margin Andreae cites volume 3, folio 478. This citation is from the German series of the Jena edition of Luther's works, a quotation from Luther's *Vom Abendmahl Christi, Bekenntnis,* of 1528. Cf. WA, 26, 410; American Edition, 37, 274.

81. Again, Andreae uses the Latin for "special terminology" and "manner of speaking."

82. This classic simile was used, e.g., by Cyril, the antagonist of Nestorius, in the fifth century; see Kelly, p. 313.

83. The Council of Ephesus met in 431 to discuss and finally to condemn Nestorianism. In connection with this condemnation the fathers at Ephesus issued the statement on the Lord's Supper to which Andreae refers; the text is given in Heinrich Denzinger, *Enchiridion symbolorum* (Freiburg: Herder, 1965), No. 262.

84. Andreae here uses the Latin word for "in reality" in his German text. The marginal note at this point reads: "The kind of abominable errors hidden under the teachings of the new Wittenbergers."

85. Arius (c. 250—c. 336) taught that Jesus Christ, as the Son of God or the Word of God, was a creature, created as a perfect being by the supreme deity; he thus denied the divinity of Christ. See Kelly, esp. pp. 226—31.

86. Sergius, a leader of the Manichaeans and a member of a related sect, the Paulicians, was a ninth-century Syrian who is alleged to have become a friend of Mohammed's and assisted him in the composition of the Koran.

87. There are a number of anti-Trinitarian theologians to whom Andreae could be referring here. Among those who had associations of one kind or another with the Reformed churches of German- or French-speaking Switzerland or in Poland are Francesco Stancaro, Gregory Paul, and George Blandratta. See George H. Williams, *The Radical Reformation* (Philadelphia: Westminster, 1962), esp. pp. 653—69. Blandratta and Francis David, who moved from Lutheranism through a commitment to a

Reformed point of view to anti-Trinitarianism, were prominent in the Reformation movement in Transylvania, in the area of the German Siebenbuergen settlements; see Williams, esp. pp. 708—32. Anti-Trinitarians in the Reformed church of the Palatinate, headquartered at Heidelberg, included Adam Neuser, pastor at St. Peter's church in Heidelberg, who was forced out of the church of the Palatinate about 1570; he eventually became a Moslem in Constantinople. Among his followers was Johannes Sylvan, who was executed for his anti-Trinitarian beliefs in 1572; see Williams, pp. 808—10.

88. Particularly since his participation in the colloquy at Worms in 1557 Andreae had been concerned about Roman Catholic charges that the Evangelicals were totally divided among themselves. In 1559 he addressed the subject at the imperial diet at Augsburg and subsequently published his *Bericht von der Einigkeit vnd Uneinigkeit der christlichen Augspurgischen Confessionsverwandten Theologen, &c.* . . . (Tuebingen: Morhart, 1560).

89. Andreae here refers to the Osiandrian controversy; see above, pp. 34—36.

90. Probably Andreae is referring to the Majoristic controversy and possibly to the controversies over Law and Gospel; see Introduction, pp. 26—27, 31—34.